ART & FEAR

ART & FEAR

*Observations
On the Perils (and Rewards)
of Artmaking*

DAVID BAYLES
TED ORLAND

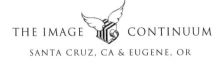

THE IMAGE CONTINUUM
SANTA CRUZ, CA & EUGENE, OR

Library of Congress Cataloging-in-Publication Data

Bayles, David.

Art & Fear:
Observations on the Perils (and Rewards) of Artmaking

p.   cm.
ISBN 978-0-9614547-3-9

1. Artists – Psychology. 2. Creation (Literary, artistic, etc.)
3. Artist's block. 4. Fear of failure.

I. Orland, Ted   II. Title.   III. Title: Art & Fear.

N71.B37   1993   93-27513
701'.15 – dc20   CIP

Book Design by Ted Orland

Printed by McNaughton & Gunn, Printers,
with special thanks to Karl Frauhammer

Distributed to the Trade by
Consortium Book Sales & Distribution, Inc.
(800) 283-3572

CAPRA PRESS EDITION
Twelve printings between March 1994 & November 2000

IMAGE CONTINUUM PRESS EDITION
First Printing, January 2001
2nd & 3rd Printings 2002
4th & 5th Printings 2004
6th Printing 2005
7th Printing 2007
8th Printing 2008

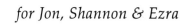

for Jon, Shannon & Ezra

CONTENTS

PART I

CONTENTS

PART II

INTRODUCTION

THIS IS A BOOK ABOUT MAKING ART. Ordinary art. Ordinary art means something like: all art *not* made by Mozart. After all, art is rarely made by Mozart-like people — essentially (statistically speaking) there *aren't* any people like that. But while geniuses may get made once-a-century or so, good art gets made all the time. Making art is a common and intimately human activity, filled with all the perils (and rewards) that accompany any worthwhile effort. The difficulties artmakers face are not remote and heroic, but universal and familiar.

This, then, is a book for the rest of us. Both authors are working artists, grappling daily with the problems of making art in the real world. The observations we make here are drawn from personal experience, and relate more closely to the needs of artists than to the interests of viewers. This book is about what it feels like to sit in your studio or classroom, at your wheel or keyboard, easel or camera, trying to do the work you need to do. It is about committing your future to your own hands, placing Free Will above predestination, choice above chance. It is about finding your own work.

David Bayles
Ted Orland

PART I

Writing is easy:
all you do is sit staring at a blank sheet of paper
until the drops of blood form on your forehead.
— Gene Fowler

I.

THE NATURE OF THE PROBLEM

Life is short, art long, opportunity fleeting,
experience treacherous, judgement difficult.
— Hippocrates (460-400 B.C.)

MAKING ART IS DIFFICULT. We leave drawings unfinished and stories unwritten. We do work that does not feel like our own. We repeat ourselves. We stop before we have mastered our materials, or continue on long after their potential is exhausted. Often the work we have not done seems more real in our minds than the pieces we have completed. And so questions arise: *How does art get done? Why, often, does it* not *get done? And what is the nature of the difficulties that stop so many who start?*

These questions, which seem so timeless, may actually be particular to our age. It may have been easier to paint bison on the cave walls long ago than to write this (or any other) sentence today. Other people, in other times and places, had some robust institutions

1

to shore them up: witness the Church, the clan, ritual, tradition. It's easy to imagine that artists doubted their calling less when working in the service of God than when working in the service of self.

Not so today. Today almost no one feels shored up. Today artwork does not emerge from a secure common ground: the bison on the wall is someone else's magic. Making art now means working in the face of uncertainty; it means living with doubt and contradiction, doing something no one much cares whether you do, and for which there may be neither audience nor reward. Making the work you want to make means setting aside these doubts so that you may see clearly what you have done, and thereby see where to go next. Making the work you want to make means finding nourishment within the work itself. This is not the Age of Faith, Truth and Certainty.

Yet even the notion that you have a say in this process conflicts with the prevailing view of artmaking today —namely, that art rests fundamentally upon talent, and that talent is a gift randomly built into some people and not into others. In common parlance, either you have it or you don't — great art is a product of genius, good art a product of near-genius (which Nabokov likened to *Near-Beer*), and so on down the line to pulp romances and paint-by-the-numbers. This view is inherently fatalistic — even if it's true, it's fatalistic — and offers no useful encouragement to those who would make art. Personally, we'll side with Conrad's view of fatalism: namely, that it is a species of fear — the fear that your fate *is* in your own hands, but that your hands are weak.

But while talent — not to mention fate, luck and tragedy — all play their role in human destiny, they hardly rank as dependable tools for advancing your own art on a day-to-day basis. Here in the day-to-day world (which is, after all, the only one we live in), the job of getting on with your work turns upon making some basic assumptions about human nature, assumptions that place the power (and hence the responsibility) for your actions in your own hands. Some of these can be stated directly:

A FEW ASSUMPTIONS

ARTMAKING INVOLVES SKILLS THAT CAN BE LEARNED. The conventional wisdom here is that while "craft" can be taught, "art" remains a magical gift bestowed only by the gods. Not so. In large measure becoming an artist consists of learning to accept yourself, which makes your work personal, and in following your own voice, which makes your work distinctive. Clearly, these qualities *can* be nurtured by others. Even talent is rarely distinguishable, over the long run, from perseverance and lots of hard work. It's true that every few years the authors encounter some beginning photography student whose first-semester prints appear as finely crafted as any Ansel Adams might have made. And it's true that a natural gift like that (especially coming at the fragile early learning stage) returns priceless encouragement to its maker. But all that has nothing to do with artistic content. Rather, it simply points up the fact that most of us (including Adams himself!) had to work years to perfect our art.

ART IS MADE BY ORDINARY PEOPLE. Creatures having only virtues can hardly be imagined making art. It's difficult to picture the Virgin Mary painting landscapes. Or Batman throwing pots. The flawless creature wouldn't *need* to make art. And so, ironically, the ideal artist is scarcely a theoretical figure at all. If art is made by ordinary people, then you'd have to allow that the ideal artist would be an ordinary person too, with the whole usual mixed bag of traits that real human beings possess. This is a giant hint about art, because it suggests that our flaws and weaknesses, while often obstacles to our getting work done, are a source of strength as well. Something about making art has to do with overcoming things, giving us a clear opportunity for doing things in ways we have always known we should do them.

MAKING ART AND VIEWING ART ARE DIFFERENT AT THEIR CORE. The sane human being is satisfied that the best he/she can do at any given moment is the best he/she can do at any given moment. That belief, if widely embraced, would make this book unnecessary, false, or both. Such sanity is, unfortunately, rare. Making art provides uncomfortably accurate feedback about the gap that inevitably exists between what you intended to do, and what you did. In fact, if artmaking did not tell you (the maker) so enormously much about yourself, then making art that matters to you would be impossible. To all viewers but yourself, what matters is the product: the finished artwork. To you, and you alone, what matters is the process: the experience of shaping that artwork. The viewers' concerns are not your concerns (although it's dangerously easy to adopt their attitudes.) Their job is whatever it is: to be moved by art, to be entertained by it, to make a killing off it, whatever. Your job is to learn to work on your work.

For the artist, that truth highlights a familiar and predictable corollary: artmaking can be a rather lonely, thankless affair. Virtually all artists spend some of their time (and some artists spend virtually all of their time) producing work that no one else much cares about. It just seems to come with the territory. But for some reason—self-defense, perhaps— artists find it tempting to romanticize this lack of response, often by (heroically) picturing themselves peering deeply into the underlying nature of things long before anyone else has eyes to follow.

Romantic, but wrong. The sobering truth is that the disinterest of others hardly ever reflects a gulf in vision. In fact there's generally no good reason why others *should* care about most of any one artist's work. The function of the overwhelming majority of your artwork is simply to teach you how to make the small fraction of your artwork that soars. One of the basic and difficult lessons every artist must learn is that even the failed pieces are essential. X-rays of famous paintings reveal that even master artists sometimes made basic mid-course corrections (or deleted really dumb mistakes) by overpainting the still-wet canvas. The point is that you learn how to make your work *by making your work*, and a great many of the pieces you make along the way will never stand out *as finished art*. The best you can do is make art you care about — and lots of it!

The rest is largely a matter of perseverance. Of course once you're famous, collectors and academics will circle back in droves to claim credit for spotting evidence of genius in every early piece. But until your ship comes in, the only people who will really care about your work are those who care about you personally. Those close to you know that making the work is essential to your well being. They will always care about your work, if not because it is great, then because it is yours — and this is something to be genuinely thankful for. Yet however much they love you, it still remains as true for them as for the rest of the world: learning to make your work is not their problem.

ARTMAKING HAS BEEN AROUND LONGER THAN THE ART ESTABLISHMENT. Through most of history, the people who made art never thought of themselves as making art. In fact it's quite presumable that art was being made long before the rise of consciousness, long before the pronoun "I" was ever employed. The painters of caves, quite apart from not thinking of themselves as artists, probably never thought of them*selves* at all.

What this suggests, among other things, is that the current view equating art with "self-expression" reveals more a contemporary bias in our thinking than an underlying trait of the medium. Even the separation of art from craft is largely a post-Renaissance concept, and more recent still is the notion that art transcends what you do, and represents what you are. In the past few centuries Western art has moved from unsigned tableaus of orthodox religious scenes to one-person displays of personal cosmologies. "Artist" has gradually become a form of identity which (as every artist knows) often carries with it as many drawbacks as benefits. Consider that if artist equals self, then when (inevitably) you make flawed art, you are a flawed person, and when (worse yet) you make no art, you are no person at all! It seems far healthier to sidestep that vicious spiral by accepting many paths to successful artmaking —from reclusive to flamboyant, intuitive to intellectual, folk art to fine art. One of those paths is yours.

II.

ART AND FEAR

*Artists don't get down to work
until the pain of working is exceeded
by the pain of not working.*

— Stephen DeStaebler

THOSE WHO WOULD MAKE ART might well begin by reflecting on the fate of those who preceded them: most who began, quit. It's a genuine tragedy. Worse yet, it's an unnecessary tragedy. After all, artists who continue and artists who quit share an immense field of common emotional ground. (Viewed from the outside, in fact, they're indistinguishable.) We're all subject to a familiar and universal progression of human troubles — troubles we routinely survive, but which are (oddly enough) routinely fatal to the art-making process. To survive as an artist requires confronting these troubles. Basically, those who continue to make art are those who have learned how to continue — or more precisely, have learned how to not quit.

But curiously, while artists always have a myriad of reasons to quit, they consistently wait for a handful of specific *moments* to quit. Artists quit when they convince themselves that their next effort is already doomed to fail. And artists quit when they lose the destination for their work — for the place their work *belongs*.

Virtually all artists encounter such moments. Fear that your next work will fail is a normal, recurring and generally healthy part of the artmaking cycle. It happens all the time: you focus on some new idea in your work, you try it out, run with it for awhile, reach a point of diminishing returns, and eventually decide it's not worth pursuing further. Writers even have a phrase for it — "the pen has run dry" — but all media have their equivalents. In the normal artistic cycle this just tells you that you've come full circle, back to that point where you need to begin cultivating the next new idea. But in artistic death it marks the *last* thing that happens: you play out an idea, it stops working, you put the brush down...and thirty years later you confide to someone over coffee that, well, yes, you had wanted to paint when you were much younger. Quitting is fundamentally different from *stopping*. The latter happens all the time. Quitting happens once. Quitting means not starting again — and art is all about starting again.

A second universal moment of truth for artists appears when the destination for the work is suddenly withdrawn. For veteran artists this moment usually coincides — rather perversely, we feel — with *reaching* that destination. The authors recall a mutual friend whose single-minded quest, for twenty years, was to land a one-man show at his city's major art museum. He finally got it. And never produced a serious piece of art again. There's a painful irony to stories like that, to discovering how frequently and easily success transmutes into depression. Avoiding this fate has something to do with not letting your current goal become your only goal. With individual artworks it means leaving some loose thread, some unresolved issue, to carry forward and explore in the next piece. With larger goals (like monographs or major shows) it means always carrying within you the seed crystal for your next destination. And for a few physically risky artforms (like dance), it may even mean keeping an alternative medium close by in case age or injury take you from your chosen work.

For art students, losing the destination for the work goes by another name: *Graduation*. Ask any student: For how many before them was the Graduate Show the Terminal Show? When "The Critique" is the only validated destination for work made during the first half-decade of an artist's productive life, small wonder that attrition rates spiral when that path stops. If ninety-eight percent of our *medical* students were no longer practicing medicine five years after graduation, there would be a Senate investigation, yet that proportion of art majors are routinely consigned to an early professional death. Not many people continue making art when — abruptly — their work is no longer seen, no longer exhibited, no longer commented upon, no longer encouraged. Could you?

Surprisingly, the dropout rate during school is not all that high — the real killer is the lack of any continuing support system afterwards. Perhaps then, if the outside world shows little interest in providing that support, it remains for artists themselves to do so. Viewed that way, a strategy suggests itself:

OPERATING MANUAL FOR NOT QUITTING

A. Make friends with others who make art, and share your in-progress work with each other frequently.

B. Learn to think of [A], rather than the Museum of Modern Art, as the destination of your work. (Look at it this way: If all goes well, MOMA will eventually come to *you*.)

The desire to make art begins early. Among the very young this is encouraged (or at least indulged as harmless) but the push toward a "serious" education soon exacts a heavy toll on dreams and fantasies. (Yes, the authors really have known students whose parents demanded they stop wasting their time on *art* or they could damn well pay their own tuition.) Yet for some the desire persists, and sooner or later must be addressed. And with good reason: your desire to make art — beautiful or meaningful or emotive art — is integral to your sense of who you are. Life and Art, once entwined, can quickly become inseparable; at age ninety Frank Lloyd Wright was still designing, Imogen Cunningham still photographing, Stravinsky still composing, Picasso still painting.

But if making art gives substance to your sense of self, the corresponding fear is that you're not up to the task — that you can't do it, or can't do it well, or can't do it again; or that you're not a real artist, or not a good artist, or have no talent, or have nothing to say. The line between the artist and his/her work is a fine one at best, and for the artist it feels (quite naturally) like there is no such line. Making art can feel dangerous and revealing. Making art *is* dangerous and revealing. Making art precipitates self-doubt, stirring deep waters that lay between what you know you should be, and what you fear you might be. For many people, that alone is enough to prevent their ever getting started at all — and for those who do, trouble isn't long in coming. Doubts, in fact, soon rise in swarms:

> *I'm not an artist — I'm a phony*
> *I have nothing worth saying*
> *I'm not sure what I'm doing*
> *Other people are better than I am*
> *I'm only a [student/physicist/mother/whatever]*
> *I've never had a real exhibit*
> *No one understands my work*
> *No one likes my work*
> *I'm no good*

Yet viewed objectively, these fears obviously have less to do with art than they do with the artist. And even less to do with individual artworks. After all, in making art you bring your highest skills to bear upon the materials and ideas you most care about. Art is a high calling—fears are coincidental. Coincidental, sneaky and disruptive, we might add, disguising themselves variously as laziness, resistance to deadlines, irritation with materials or surroundings, distraction over the achievements of others—indeed as anything that keeps you from giving your work your best shot. What separates artists from ex-artists is that those who challenge their fears, continue; those who don't, quit. Each step in the artmaking process puts that issue to the test.

VISION & EXECUTION

Fears arise when you look back, and they arise when you look ahead. If you're prone to disaster fantasies you may even find yourself caught in the middle, staring at your half-finished canvas and fearing both that you lack the ability to finish it, and that no one will understand it if you do.

More often, though, fears rise in those entirely appropriate (and frequently recurring) moments when vision races ahead of execution. Consider the story of the young student — well, David Bayles, to be exact — who began piano studies with a Master. After a few months' practice, David lamented to his teacher, "But I can hear the music so much better in my head than I can get out of my fingers."

To which the Master replied, "What makes you think that ever changes?"

That's why they're called Masters. When he raised David's discovery from an expression of self-doubt to a simple observation of reality, uncertainty became an asset. Lesson for the day: vision is always ahead of execution — and it *should* be. Vision, Uncertainty, and Knowledge of Materials are inevitabilities that all artists must acknowledge and learn from: vision is always ahead of execution, knowledge of materials is your contact with reality, and uncertainty is a virtue.

IMAGINATION

Imagination is in control when you begin making an object. The artwork's potential is never higher than in that magic moment when the first brushstroke is applied, the first chord struck. But as the piece grows, technique and craft take over, and imagination becomes a less useful tool. A piece grows by becoming specific. The moment Herman Melville penned the opening line, "Call me Ishmael", one actual story—*Moby Dick*—began to separate itself from a multitude of imaginable others. And so on through the following five hundred-odd pages, each successive sentence in some way had to acknowledge and relate to all that preceded. Joan Didion nailed this issue squarely (and with trademark pessimism) when she said, "What's so hard about that first sentence is that you're stuck with it. Everything else is going to flow out of that sentence. And by the time you've laid down the first *two* sentences, your options are all gone."

It's the same for all media: the first few brushstrokes to the blank canvas satisfy the requirements of many possible paintings, while the last few fit only *that* painting — they could go nowhere else. The development of an imagined piece into an actual piece is a progression of decreasing possibilities, as each step in execution reduces future options by converting one — and only one — possibility into a reality. Finally, at some point or another, the piece could not be other than it is, and it is done.

That moment of completion is also, inevitably, a moment of loss — the loss of all the other forms the imagined piece might have taken. The irony here is that the piece you make is always one step removed from what you imagined, or what else you can imagine, or what you're right on the edge of being able to imagine. Designer Charles Eames, arguably the quintessential Renaissance Man of the twentieth century, used to complain good-naturedly that he devoted only about one percent of his energy to conceiving a design — and the remaining ninety-nine percent to *holding onto it* as a project ran its course. Small surprise. After all, your imagination is free to race a hundred works ahead, conceiving pieces you could and perhaps should and maybe one day *will* execute — but not today, not in the piece at hand. All you can work on today is directly in front of you. Your job is to develop an imagination of the possible.

A finished piece is, in effect, a test of correspondence between imagination and execution. And perhaps surprisingly, the more common obstacle to achieving that correspondence is not undisciplined execution, but undisciplined imagination. It's altogether too seductive to approach your proposed work believing your materials to be more malleable than they really are, your ideas more compelling, your execution more refined. As Stanley Kunitz once commented, "The poem in the head is always perfect. Resistance begins when you try to convert it into language." And it's true, most artists don't daydream about making great art — they daydream about *having made* great art. What artist has not experienced the feverish euphoria of composing the *perfect* thumbnail sketch, first draft, negative or melody — only to run headlong into a stone wall trying to convert that tantalizing hint into the finished mural, novel, photograph, sonata. The artist's life is frustrating not because the passage is slow, but because he imagines it to be fast.

MATERIALS

The materials of art, like the thumbnail sketch, seduce us with their potential. The texture of the paper, the smell of the paint, the weight of the stone — all cast hints and innuendoes, beckoning our fantasies. In the presence of good materials, hopes grow and possibilities multiply. And with good reason: some materials are so readily charged and responsive that artists have turned to them for thousands of years, and probably will for thousands more. For many artists the response to a particular material has been intensely personal, as if the material spoke directly to them. It's been said that as a child, Pablo Casals knew from the first moment he heard the sound of a cello, that that was *his* instrument.

But where materials have potential, they also have limits. Ink wants to flow, but not across just any surface; clay wants to hold a shape, but not just any shape. And in any case, without your active participation their potential remains just that—potential. Materials are like elementary particles: charged, but indifferent. They do not listen in on your fantasies, do not get up and move in response to your idle wishes. The blunt truth is, they do precisely what your hands make them do. The paint lays exactly where you put it; the words you wrote — not the ones you needed to write or thought about writing — are the only ones that appear on the paper. In the words of Ben Shahn, "The painter who stands before an empty canvas must think in terms of paint."

What counts, in making art, is the actual fit between the contents of your head and the qualities of your materials. The knowledge you need to make that fit comes from noticing what really happens as you work — the way the materials respond, and the way that response (and resistance) suggest new ideas to you. It's those real and ordinary changes that matter. Art is about carrying things out, and materials are what *can* be carried out. Because they are real, they are reliable.

UNCERTAINTY

Your materials are, in fact, one of the few elements of artmaking you can reasonably hope to control. As for everything else—well, conditions are never perfect, sufficient knowledge rarely at hand, key evidence always missing, and support notoriously fickle. All that you do will inevitably be flavored with uncertainty — uncertainty about what you have to say, about whether the materials are right, about whether the piece should be long or short, indeed about whether you'll ever be satisfied with *anything* you make. Photographer Jerry Uelsmann once gave a slide lecture in which he showed every single image he had created in the span of one year: some hundred-odd pieces — all but about ten of which he judged insufficient and destroyed without ever exhibiting. Tolstoy, in the Age Before Typewriters, re-wrote *War & Peace* eight times and was still revising galley proofs as it finally rolled onto the press. William Kennedy gamely admitted that he re-wrote his own novel *Legs* eight times, and that "seven times it came out no good. Six times it was especially no good. The seventh time out it was pretty good, though it was way too long. My son was six years old by then and so was my novel and they were both about the same height."

It is, in short, the normal state of affairs. The truth is that the piece of art which seems so profoundly right in its finished state may earlier have been only inches or seconds away from total collapse. Lincoln doubted his capacity to express what needed to be said at Gettysburg, yet pushed ahead anyway, knowing he was doing the best he could to present the ideas he needed to share. It's always like that. Art is like beginning a sentence before you know its ending. The risks are obvious: you may never get to the end of the sentence at all — or having gotten there, you may not have said anything. This is probably not a good idea in public speaking, but it's an excellent idea in making art.

In making art you need to give yourself room to respond authentically, both to your subject matter and to your materials. Art happens *between* you and something — a subject, an idea, a technique — and both you and that something need to be free to move. Many fiction writers, for instance, discover early on that making detailed plot outlines is an exercise in futility; as actual writing progresses, characters increasingly take on a life of their own, sometimes to the point that the writer is as surprised as the eventual reader by what their creations say and do. Lawrence Durrell likened the process to driving construction stakes in the ground: you plant a stake, run fifty yards ahead a plant another, and pretty soon you know which way the road will run. E.M. Forster recalled that when he began writing *A Passage To India* he knew that the Malabar Caves would play a central role in the novel, that something important would surely happen there — it's just that he wasn't sure what it would be.

Control, apparently, is not the answer. People who need certainty in their lives are less likely to make art that is risky, subversive, complicated, iffy, suggestive or spontaneous. What's really needed is nothing more than a broad sense of what you are looking for, some strategy for how to find it, and an overriding willingness to embrace mistakes and surprises along the way. Simply put, making art is chancy — it doesn't mix well with predictability. Uncertainty is the essential, inevitable and all-pervasive companion to your desire to make art. And tolerance for uncertainty is the prerequisite to succeeding.

III.

FEARS ABOUT YOURSELF

We have met the enemy and he is us.

— Pogo

A HEAD LIES A BROAD EXPANSE of river, flowing rapidly. The oarsman, only recently learning his skill, nervously maneuvers to avoid the one and only rock breaking the surface downstream, dead center, smooth current to either side. You watch from shore. The oarsman zigs left. Zigs right. And then crashes directly into the rock. When you act out of fear, your fears come true.

Fears about artmaking fall into two families: fears about yourself, and fears about your reception by others. In a general way, fears about yourself prevent you from doing your *best* work, while fears about your reception by others prevent you from doing your *own* work. Both families surface in many forms, some of which you may find all too familiar. Try this sampler...

PRETENDING

The fear that you're only pretending to do art is the (readily predictable) consequence of doubting your own artistic credentials. After all, you know better than anyone else the accidental nature of much that appears in your art, not to mention all those elements you know originated with others (and even some you never even intended but which the audience has read into your work). From there it's only a short hop to feeling like you're just going through the motions of being an artist. It's easy to imagine that *real* artists know what they're doing, and that they—unlike you—are entitled to feel good about themselves and their art. Fear that you are not a real artist causes you to undervalue your work.

The chasm widens even further when your work isn't going well, when happy accidents aren't happening or hunches aren't paying off. If you buy into the premise that art can be made only by people who are extra-ordinary, such down periods only serve to confirm that you *aren't*.

Before chucking it all for a day job, however, consider the dynamics at work here. Both making art and viewing art require an ongoing investment of energy—lots of energy. In moments of weakness, the myth of the extraordinary provides the excuse for an artist to quit trying to make art, and the excuse for a viewer to quit trying to understand it.

Meanwhile artists who do continue often become perilously self-conscious about their artmaking. If you doubt this could be a problem, just try working intuitively (or spontaneously) while self-consciously weighing the effect of your every action. The increasing prevalence of reflexive art — art that looks inward, taking itself as its subject — may to some degree simply illustrate attempts by artists to turn this obstacle to their advantage. Art-that's-about-art has in turn spawned a whole school of art criticism built around the demonstrably true (but limited) premise that artists continually "re-define" art through their work. This approach treats "what art is" as a legitimate, serious and even thorny topic, but expends little energy on the question of "what art *making* is".

Clearly something's come unbalanced here. After all, if there were some ongoing redefinition of "what chess is", you'd probably feel a little uneasy trying to play chess. Of course you could always stick with the game by limiting yourself to a few easy moves you've seen work for others. Then again you might conclude that since you weren't sure yourself what chess was, you weren't a *real* chess player and were only faking it when you moved the pieces around. You might secretly come to believe that you deserve to lose. In fact, you might even quit playing entirely. If the preceding scenario sounds farfetched *vis-a-vis* chess, it remains discouragingly common *vis-a-vis* art.

But while you may feel you're just pretending that you're an artist, there's no way to pretend you're making art. Go ahead, try writing a story while pretending you're writing a story. Not possible. Your work may not be what curators want to exhibit or publishers want to publish, but those are different issues entirely. You make good work by (among other things) making lots of work that isn't very good, and gradually weeding out the parts that aren't good, the parts that aren't yours. It's called feedback, and it's the most direct route to learning about your own vision. It's also called doing your work. After all, *someone* has to do your work, and you're the closest person around.

TALENT

Talent, in common parlance, is "what comes easily". So sooner or later, inevitably, you reach a point where the work doesn't come easily, and — *Aha!*, it's just as you feared!

Wrong. By definition, *whatever* you have is exactly what you need to produce your best work. There is probably no clearer waste of psychic energy than worrying about how much talent you have — and probably no worry more common. This is true even among artists of considerable accomplishment.

Talent, if it is anything, is a gift, and nothing of the artist's own making. This idea is hardly new: Plato maintained that all art is a gift from the gods, channeled through artists who are "out of their mind" — quite literally, in Plato's view — when making art. Plato, however, is not the only philosopher on the block; while his description correlates well with the functioning of the Oracle at Delphi, idiot savants, and certain TV evangelists, it's difficult to reconcile with most real world events.

Were talent a prerequisite, then the better the art-work, the easier it would have been to make. But alas, the fates are rarely so generous. For every artist who has developed a mature vision with grace and speed, countless others have laboriously nurtured their art through fertile periods and dry spells, through false starts and breakaway bursts, through successive and significant changes of direction, medium, and subject matter. Talent may get someone off the starting blocks faster, but without a sense of direction or a goal to strive for, it won't count for much. The world is filled with people who were given great natural gifts, sometimes conspicuously flashy gifts, yet never produce anything. And when that happens, the world soon ceases to care whether they are talented.

Even at best talent remains a constant, and those who rely upon that gift alone, without developing further, peak quickly and soon fade to obscurity. Examples of genius only accentuate that truth. Newspapers love to print stories about five-year-old musical prodigies giving solo recitals, but you rarely read about one going on to become a Mozart. The point here is that whatever his initial gift, Mozart was also an artist who learned to work on his work, and thereby improved. In that respect he shares common ground with the rest of us. Artists get better by sharpening their skills or by acquiring new ones; they get better by learning to work, and by learning *from* their work. They commit themselves to the work of their heart, and act upon that commitment. So when you ask, "Then why doesn't it come easily for me?", the answer is probably, "Because making art is hard!" What you end up caring about is what you *do*, not whether the doing came hard or easy.

A BRIEF DIGRESSION
IN WHICH THE AUTHORS ATTEMPT
TO ANSWER (OR DEFLECT) AN OBJECTION:

Q: Aren't you ignoring the fact that people differ radically in their abilities?
A: No.
Q: But if people differ, and each of them were to make their best work, would not the more gifted make better work, and the less gifted, less?
A: Yes. And wouldn't that be a nice planet to live on?

Talent is a snare and a delusion. In the end, the practical questions about talent come down to these: Who cares? Who would know? and What difference would it make? And the practical answers are: Nobody, Nobody, and None.

PERFECTION

The ceramics teacher announced on opening day that he was dividing the class into two groups. All those on the left side of the studio, he said, would be graded solely on the *quantity* of work they produced, all those on the right solely on its *quality*. His procedure was simple: on the final day of class he would bring in his bathroom scales and weigh the work of the "quantity" group: fifty pounds of pots rated an "A", forty pounds a "B", and so on. Those being graded on "quality", however, needed to produce only one pot — albeit a perfect one — to get an "A". Well, came grading time and a curious fact emerged: the works of highest quality were all produced by the group being graded for quantity. It seems that while the "quantity" group was busily churning out piles of work — and learning from their mistakes — the "quality" group had sat theorizing about perfection, and in the end had little more to show for their efforts than grandiose theories and a pile of dead clay.

If you think good work is somehow synonymous with perfect work, you are headed for big trouble. Art is human; error is human; *ergo,* art is error. Inevitably, your work (like, uh, the preceding syllogism...) will be flawed. Why? Because you're a human being, and only human beings, warts and all, make art. Without warts it is not clear what you would be, but clearly you wouldn't be one of us.

Nonetheless, the belief persists among some artists (and lots of ex-artists) that doing art means doing things flawlessly — ignoring the fact that this prerequisite would disqualify most existing works of art. Indeed, it seems vastly more plausible to advance the counter-principle, namely that imperfection is not only a common ingredient in art, but very likely an essential ingredient. Ansel Adams, never one to mistake precision for perfection, often recalled the old adage that "the perfect is the enemy of the good", his point being that if he waited for everything in the scene to be exactly right, he'd probably never make a photograph.

Adams was right: to require perfection is to invite paralysis. The pattern is predictable: as you see error in what you have done, you steer your work toward what you imagine you can do perfectly. You cling ever more tightly to what you already know you can do — away from risk and exploration, and possibly further from the work of your heart. You find reasons to procrastinate, since to *not* work is to not make mistakes. Believing that artwork should be perfect, you gradually become convinced that you cannot make such work. (You are correct.) Sooner or later, since you cannot do what you are trying to do, you quit. And in one of those perverse little ironies of life, only the pattern itself achieves perfection — a perfect death spiral: you misdirect your work; you stall; you quit.

To demand perfection is to deny your ordinary (and universal) humanity, as though you would be better off without it. Yet this humanity is the ultimate source of your work; your perfectionism denies you the very thing you need to get your work done. Getting on with your work requires a recognition that perfection itself is (paradoxically) a flawed concept. For Albert Einstein, even the seemingly perfect construct of mathematics yielded to his observation that "As far as the laws of mathematics refer to reality, they are not certain; and as far as they are certain, they do not refer to reality." For Charles Darwin, evolution lay revealed when a perfect survival strategy for one generation became, in a changing world, a liability for its offspring. For you, the seed for your next art work lies embedded in the imperfections of your current piece. Such imperfections (or *mistakes*, if you're feeling particularly depressed about them today) are your guides—valuable, reliable, objective, non-judgmental guides—to matters you need to reconsider or develop further. It is precisely this interaction between the ideal and the real that locks your art into the real world, and gives meaning to both.

ANNIHILATION

For most artists, hitting a dry spell in their artmaking would be a serious blow; for a few it would amount to annihilation. Some artists identify so closely with their own work that were they to cease producing, they fear they would be nothing—that they would cease *existing*. In the words of John Barth, "It's Scheherazade's terror: the terror that comes from the literal or metaphorical

31

equating of telling stories with living, with life itself. I understand that metaphor to the marrow of my bones."

Some avoid this self-imposed abyss by becoming stupendously productive, churning out work in quantities that surprise even close friends (and positively unnerve envious peers!). They work passionately, as if they were possessed — and wouldn't you too, if that were all that kept the Reaper at bay?

Others, no less driven, project instead a certain no-nonsense professionalism: precise, relentless, and narrowly aimed at making art — which, indeed, they may be very good at. History records that Anthony Trollope methodically drafted exactly forty-nine pages of manuscript a week — seven pages a day — and was so obsessed with keeping to that schedule that if he finished a novel in the morning he'd pen the title for his *next* book on a new sheet and plod relentlessly ahead until he'd completed his quota for the day. And from personal experience the authors can verify that Brett Weston, a virtual case study in annihilation, for decades maintained in his home an ongoing exhibition of a dozen or more of his photographs, none of which was ever more than six months old.

Still, there must be many fates worse than the inability to stop producing art. The artist who fears annihilation may draw the connection between *doing* and *being* a little too tight, but this is really just a case of having too much of a good thing. Annihilation is an existential fear: the common — but sharply overdrawn — fear that some part of you dies when you stop making art. *And it's true.* Non-artists may not understand that, but artists themselves (especially those who are stuck) understand it all too well. The depth of your need to make things establishes the level of risk in not making them.

MAGIC

"There's a myth among amateurs, optimists and fools that beyond a certain level of achievement, famous artists retire to some kind of Elysium where criticism no longer wounds and work materializes without their effort."

— Mark Matousek

In a darkened theater the man in the tuxedo waves his hand and a pigeon appears. We call it magic. In a sunlit studio a painter waves her hand and a whole world takes form. We call it art. Sometimes the difference isn't all that clear. Imagine you've just attended an exhibition and seen work that's powerful and coherent, work that has range and purpose. The Artist's Statement framed near the door is clear: these works materialized exactly as the artist conceived them. The work is inevitable. But wait a minute — *your* work doesn't feel inevitable (you think), and so you begin to wonder: maybe making art requires some special or even magic ingredient *that you don't have.*

The belief that "real" art possesses some indefinable magic ingredient puts pressure on you to prove your work contains the same. Wrong, very wrong. Asking your work to prove anything only invites doom. Besides, if artists share any common view of magic, it is probably the fatalistic suspicion that when their own art turns out well, it's a fluke — but when it turns out poorly, it's an *omen*. Buying into magic leaves you feeling less capable each time another artist's qualities are praised. So if a critic praises Nabokov's obsession with wordplay, you begin to worry that you can't even spell "obsession". If Christo's love of process is championed, you feel guilty that you've always hated cleaning your brushes. If some art historian comments that great art is the product of especially fertile times and places, you begin to think maybe you need to move to New York.

Admittedly, artmaking probably does require *something* special, but just what that something might be has remained remarkably elusive — elusive enough to suggest that it may be something particular to each artist, rather than universal to them all. (Or even, perhaps, that it's all nothing more than the art world's variation on The Emperor's New Suit of Clothes.) But the important point here is not that you have — or don't have — what other artists have, but rather that it doesn't matter. Whatever they have is something needed to do their work — it wouldn't help you in your work even if you had it. Their magic is theirs. You don't lack it. You don't need it. It has nothing to do with you. Period.

EXPECTATIONS

Hovering out there somewhere between cause and effect, between fears about self and fears about others, lie expectations. Being one of the higher brain functions (as our neocortex modestly calls itself), expectations provide a means to merge imagination with calculation. But it's a delicate balance — lean too far one way and your head fills with unworkable fantasies, too far the other and you spend your life generating "To Do" lists.

Worse yet, expectations drift into fantasies all too easily. At a recent writers' workshop, the instructor labored heroically to keep the discussion centered upon issues of craft (as yet unlearned), while the writers (as yet unpublished) labored equally to divert the focus with questions about royalties, movie rights and sequels.

Given a small kernel of reality and any measure of optimism, nebulous expectations whisper to you that the work will soar, that it will become easy, that it will make itself. And verily, now and then the sky opens and the work *does* make itself. Unreal expectations are easy to come by, both from emotional needs and from the hope or memory of periods of wonder. Unfortunately, expectations based on illusion lead almost always to disillusionment.

Conversely, expectations based on the work itself are the most useful tool the artist possesses. What you need to know about the next piece is contained in the last piece. The place to learn about your materials is in the last use of your materials. The place to learn about your execution is in your execution. The best information about what you love is in your last contact with what you love. Put simply, your work is your guide: a complete, comprehensive, limitless reference book on your work. There is no other such book, and it is yours alone. It functions this way for no one else. Your fingerprints are all over your work, and you alone know how they got there. Your work tells you about your working methods, your discipline, your strengths and weaknesses, your habitual gestures, your willingness to embrace.

The lessons you are meant to learn are in your work. To see them, you need only look at the work clearly — without judgement, without need or fear, without wishes or hopes. Without emotional expectations. Ask your work what it needs, not what you need. Then set aside your fears and listen, the way a good parent listens to a child.

IV.

FEARS ABOUT OTHERS

"Don't look back —
something might be gaining on you."
— Satchel Paige

ART IS OFTEN MADE IN ABANDONMENT, emerging unbidden in moments of selfless rapport with the materials and ideas we care about. In such moments we leave no space for others. That's probably as it should be. Art, after all, rarely emerges from committees.

But while others' reactions need not cause problems for the artist, they usually *do*. The problems arise when we confuse others' priorities with our own. We carry real and imagined critics with us constantly — a veritable babble of voices, some remembered, some prophesied, and each eager to comment on all we do. Beyond that, even society's general notions about artmaking confront the artist with paralyzing contradictions. As an artist you're expected to make each successive piece uniquely new and different — yet reassuringly familiar when set

37

alongside your earlier work. You're expected to make art that's intimately (perhaps even painfully) personal — yet alluring and easily grasped by an audience that has likely never known you personally.

When the work goes well, we keep such inner distractions at bay, but in times of uncertainty or need, we begin listening. We abdicate artistic decision-making to others when we fear that the work itself will not bring us the understanding, acceptance and approval we seek. For students in academic settings, this trouble is a near certainty; you know (and you are correct) that if you steer your work along certain paths, three units of "A" can be yours. Outside academia, approval may be clothed in loftier terms — critical recognition, shows, fellowships — but the mechanism remains the same.

With commercial art this issue is often less troublesome since approval from the client is primary, and other rewards appropriately secondary. But for most art there is no client, and in making it you lay bare a truth you perhaps never anticipated: that by your very contact with what you love, you have exposed yourself to the world. How could you *not* take criticism of that work personally?

UNDERSTANDING

We all learn at a young age the perils of being perceived as different. We learn that others have the power to single out, to ridicule, to turn away from and to *mark* the one who is different. Choose your own memories, but one way or another we've all felt the hurt of the little boy who wanted to write poems, or the little girl who tried to join the sandlot ball game.

As an artist, you learn these lessons all over again — with a vengeance. In following the path of your heart, the chances are that your work will not be understandable to others. At least not immediately, and not to a wide audience. When the author fed his computer the question, "What works?", a curious pattern emerged: a consistent delay of about five years between the making of any given negative, and the time when prints from that negative began selling. In fact, one now-popular work was first reproduced in a critical review to illustrate how much *weaker* the then-new work had become. Performing artists face the added, real-time terror of receiving an instant verdict on their work in person — like the conductor being pummeled with a barrage of rotten fruit halfway through the Paris premier of *Rite of Spring,* or Bob Dylan being hooted off the stage the first time he appeared live with an electric guitar. No wonder artists so often harbor a depressing sense that their work is going downhill: at any give moment the older work is always more attractive, always better understood.

This is not good. After all, wanting to be understood is a basic need — an affirmation of the humanity you share with everyone around you. The risk is fearsome: in making your real work you hand the audience the power to deny the understanding you seek; you hand them the power to say, "you're not like us; you're weird; you're crazy."

And admittedly, there's always a chance they may be right — your work may provide clear evidence that you are different, that you are alone. After all, artists themselves rarely serve as role models of normalcy. As Ben Shahn rather wryly commented, "It may be a point of great pride to have a Van Gogh on the living room wall, but the prospect of having Van Gogh himself in the living room would put a great many devoted art lovers to rout." Put that way, platitudes about the virtues of individuality sound distinctly hollow. Just how unintelligible your art — or you — appear to others may be something you don't really want to confront, at least not all that quickly.

What is sometimes needed is simply an insulating period, a gap of pure time between the making of your art, and the time when you share it with outsiders. Andrew Wyeth pursued his *Helga* series privately for years, working at his own pace, away from the spotlight of criticism and suggestion that would otherwise have accompanied the release of each new piece in the series. Such respites also, perhaps, allow the finished work time to find its rightful place in the artist's heart and mind — in short, a chance to be understood better by the maker. Then when the time comes for others to judge the work, their reaction (whatever it may be) is less threatening.

Conversely, catering to fears of being misunderstood leaves you dependent upon your audience. In the simplest yet most deadly scenario, ideas are diluted to what you imagine your audience can imagine, leading to work that is condescending, arrogant, or both. Worse yet, you discard your own highest vision in the process.

In the face of such pressures, it's heartening to find contemporary role models even among those who made it their goal to address the mass audience. Charles Eames and Jacob Bronowski consistently placed trust in the potential of their audience to grow and benefit from new ideas. Eames once designed a museum exhibit that featured a fifteen foot long wall chart (set in textbook-sized type and equally small pictures) delineating the entire history of mathematics. When asked who on earth would possibly read the whole wall, he calmly replied that each person would probably absorb about as much as he/she were able to, and just slough off the rest. And, he added, that would include some who would make connections between the data beyond what Eames himself could perceive.

ACCEPTANCE

For the artist, the issue of acceptance begins as one simple, haunting question: When your work is counted, will it be counted *as art?* It's a basic question, with antecedents stretching back to childhood. (Remember those dreaded playground rituals, when you'd feel badly enough if you weren't the first one chosen for the softball team, but would rather die than not be chosen at all?)

If the need for acceptance is the need to have your work accepted as art, then the accompanying fear is finding it dismissed as craft, hobby, decoration—or as nothing at all. In 1937, when Beaumont Newhall wrote the first substantive account of the history of photography (titled, logically enough, *The History of Photography*), he picked a select number of artists to praise or criticize. As it turned out, the photographers hurt by Newhall's book were not those he damned, but those he left out entirely. In the public's mind, the former at least became part of "the history of photography", while the latter ceased to exist entirely! Literally decades passed before some talented "outsies" began receiving recognition for the work they produced in those early days. That example is extreme, but the general caveat still applies: acceptance and approval are powers held by others, whether they be friends, classmates, curators...or author of the definitive history of your chosen medium.

At some point the need for acceptance may well collide head-on with the need to do your own work. It's too bad, since the request itself seems so reasonable: you want to do your own work, and you want acceptance for that. It's the ballad of the cowboy and the mountain man, the myth of artistic integrity and Sesame Street: sing the song of your heart, and sooner or later the world will accept and reward the authentic voice. Jaded sophisticates laugh at this belief, but usually buy into it along with everyone else anyway.

In the non-art world, this belief system is a driving mechanism behind the American Dream — and the Mid-Life Crisis. In the art world, it's a primary buffer against disillusionment. After all, the world does (in large measure) reward authentic work. The problem is not absolute, but temporal: by the time your reward arrives, you may no longer be around to collect it. Ask Schubert.

There's a fairly straightforward explanation for this: at any given moment, the world offers vastly more support to work it already understands — namely, art that's already been around for a generation or a century. Expressions of truly new ideas often fail to qualify as even bad art — they're simply viewed as no art at all. Stravinski's *Firebird*, today considered one of the more lushly melodic of twentieth century symphonic pieces, was rejected as sheer cacophony when first performed. Robert Frank's *The Americans*, now considered a seminal turning point in American photography, was at the time of its publication largely ignored by a press and public that couldn't decipher its dark and gritty vision. It's a dreary tradition: artists from Atget to Weegee were ignored through most of their careers because the work they produced didn't fit within the established definition of art.

For the artist, the dilemma seems obvious: risk rejection by exploring new worlds, or court acceptance by following well-explored paths. Needless to say, the latter strategy is the overwhelming drug of choice where acceptance is the primary goal. Make work that *looks like* art, and acceptance is automatic.

Surprisingly, however, this is not always a bad thing. At least for the novitiate, some period of artistic recapitulation is both inevitable and, by most accounts, beneficial. On both intellectual and technical grounds, it's wise to remain on good terms with your artistic heritage, lest you devote several incarnations to re-inventing the wheel. But once having allowed for that, the far greater danger is not that the artist will fail to learn anything from the past, but will fail to teach anything new to the future.

Recent photo history offers a textbook example of the perils that success itself can lay in the path of continued artistic growth. In the first third of this century, Edward Weston, Ansel Adams and a few fellow travellers turned the then-prevailing world of soft-focus photographic art upside down. They did so by developing a visual philosophy that justified sharply-focused images, and introduced the natural landscape as a subject for photographic art. It took decades for their viewpoint to filter into public consciousness, but it sure has now: pictures appearing in anything from cigarette ads to Sierra Club books owe their current acceptance to those once-controversial images. Indeed, that vision has so pervasively become ours that people photographing vacation scenery today often do so with the hope that if everything turns out just right, the result will not simply look like a landscape, it will look like *an Ansel Adams photograph* of the landscape.

This too will pass, of course. In fact, artistically speaking, it *has* passed. The unfolding over time of a great idea is like the growth of a fractal crystal, allowing details and refinements to multiply endlessly — but only in ever-decreasing scale. Eventually (perhaps by the early 1960's) those who stepped forward to carry the West Coast Landscape Photography banner were not producing art, so much as re-producing the history of art. Separated two or three generations from the forces that spawned the vision they championed, they were left making images of experiences they never quite had. If you find yourself caught in similar circumstances, we modestly offer this bit of cowboy wisdom: When your horse dies, get off.

Cowboy wisdom notwithstanding, the Weston/Adams vision continues to support a sizable cottage industry of artists and teachers even today. But this security carries a price: risk-taking is discouraged, artistic development stunted, and personal style sublimated to fit a pre-existing mold. Only those who commit to following their own artistic path can look back and see this issue in clear perspective: the real question about acceptance is not whether your work will be viewed as art, but whether it will be viewed as *your* art.

APPROVAL

The difference between acceptance and approval is subtle, but distinct. Acceptance means having your work counted as the real thing; approval means having people *like it*.

It's not unusual to receive one without the other. Norman Rockwell's work was enormously well-liked during his lifetime, but received little critical respect. A generation or two earlier there was widespread agreement that John Singer Sargent was good, but that for various reasons his work didn't really count. On the flip side, every season brings a small bundle of films and plays that garner rave critical reviews while on their way to becoming box office disasters.

That this dichotomy exists is undeniable; whether it need be destructive is an open question. Both acceptance and approval are, quite plainly, audience-related issues. In a healthy environment, good work would get recognition; if your only validation is internal, society has failed. Sounds straightforward enough, but society is hardly a monolith—it harbors many environments, some repressive to the artist, others supportive. For artists who thrive on confrontation, rejection is not a problem, but for many others the constant wear and tear takes a toll. For those artists, survival means finding an environment where art is valued and artmaking encouraged.

In a supportive environment—one found, more often than not, within the artistic community itself—approval and acceptance often become linked, even indistinguishable. The operative criteria for this rather select audience is typified by Ed Ruscha's remark, "There are only artists and hacks," or James Thurber's observation, "There's no such thing as good art or bad art. There's only Art—and damn little of it!"

But be forewarned: this approach can be harsh. There's a story (perhaps apocryphal) of the Master who was asked to judge a competition for twenty young pianists by rating their performance on a scale of 1-to-100. Afterwards, his tally sheet revealed he had awarded two pianists a perfect hundred — and given the rest a zero. When the sponsors protested, he replied bluntly, "Either you can play or you can't."

Filmmaker Lou Stoumen tells the painfully *un*-apocryphal story about hand-carrying his first film (produced while he was still a student) to the famed teacher and film theorist Slavko Vorkapitch. The teacher watched the entire film in silence, and as the viewing ended rose and left the room without uttering a word. Stoumen, more than a bit shaken, ran out after him and asked, "But what did you think of my film?"

Replied Vorkapitch, "What film?"

The lesson here is simply that courting approval, even that of peers, puts a dangerous amount of power in the hands of the audience. Worse yet, the audience is seldom in a position to grant (or withhold) approval on the one issue that really counts — namely, whether or not you're making progress in your work. They're in a good position to comment on how they're moved (or challenged or entertained) by the finished product, but have little knowledge or interest in your *process*. Audience comes later. The only pure communication is between you and your work.

V.

FINDING YOUR WORK

You could not step twice into the same river;
for other waters are ever flowing on to you.
— Heraclitus (ca. 540 – 480 BC)

THE WORLD DISPLAYS PERFECT NEUTRALITY on whether we achieve any outward manifestation of our inner desires. But not art. Art is exquisitely responsive. Nowhere is feedback so absolute as in the making of art. The work we make, even if unnoticed and undesired by the world, vibrates in perfect harmony to everything we put into it — or withhold from it. In the outside world there may be no reaction to what we do; in our artwork there is nothing but reaction.

The breathtakingly wonderful thing about this reaction is its truthfulness. Look at your work and it tells you how it is when you hold back or when you embrace. When you are lazy, your art is lazy; when you hold back, it holds back; when you hesitate, it stands there staring, hands in its pockets. But when you commit, it comes on like blazes.

Recently, out of pleasure alone, an accomplished visual artist took up dance. Never before experiencing an artform so purely physical, she threw herself into it. Her involvement became intense: more classes, more practice, more commitment, longer hours. She excelled. Then one day several months into it, her instructor asked her to consider joining a performing troupe. She froze. Her dancing fell apart. She became stiff and self-conscious. She got serious, or serious in a different way. She didn't feel she was good enough, and her dancing promptly was not good enough. She got frustrated and depressed enough that she had to quit for a few weeks to sort things out. More recently, back to work on new but shaky ground, she's having to teach herself to enjoy working hard for others at the art she previously enjoyed passionately for herself.

In the ideal — that is to say, *real* — artist, fears not only continue to exist, they exist side by side with the desires that complement them, perhaps drive them, certainly feed them. Naive passion, which promotes work done in ignorance of obstacles, becomes — with courage — informed passion, which promotes work done in full acceptance of those obstacles.

Foremost among those obstacles is uncertainty. We all know the feeling of finished art that rides from within its uncertainties. Music, with its dense structure and built-in abstraction, offers the clearest examples. In performances of really wonderful music there's an ongoing tension between where the musical line is, and where we know it needs to go. We're uncertain (momentarily) just how the fugue can be resolved, even as (simultaneously) we know it will be. What is more difficult to describe is the state of mind held by the artist while working on the piece. Most artists keep a well-rehearsed speech close at hand for fielding the familiar request to explain a finished piece. But if asked to describe how it felt *during* the artmaking — well, that often comes out a bit like Dorothy trying to describe the Land of Oz to Auntie Em. Between the initial idea and the finished piece lies a gulf we can see across, but never fully chart. The truly special moments in artmaking lie in those moments when concept is converted to reality — those moments when the gulf is being crossed. Precise descriptions fail, but it connects to that wonderful condition in which the work seems to make itself and the artist serves only as guide or mediator, allowing all things to be possible.

All things considered, in most matters of art it is more nourishing to be a maker than a viewer. But not in all matters. When it comes to the *range* of art we can usefully engage, some benefits that flow freely to art viewers remain tantalizingly inaccessible to art makers. As a listener you can be transported to authentic ecstasy and catharsis by a performance of the Bach B-minor Mass, but as a maker you cannot compose even the most trivial piece of authentic baroque music. As a viewer you can feel the charge in the presence of the Plains Indian medicine bundle, but as a twentieth century artist you could not begin to make one yourself.

Your reach as a viewer is vastly greater than your reach as a maker. The art you can experience may have originated a thousand miles away or a thousand years ago, but the art you can *make* is irrevocably bound to the times and places of your life. Limited by the very ground on which you stand. Without a broadly shared belief in the symbolism of the Cross and the promise of Heaven above, the cruciform design and towering spires of the great European cathedrals would have made no sense whatsoever. Seen against the vast sweep of history, it is only for brief moments that particular events and beliefs carry the power to compel us to build cathedrals or write fugues. And it's just as likely that a similarly narrow (albeit different) range of beliefs drives all that is authentically available to us in this moment. Decisive works of art participate directly in the fabric of history surrounding their maker. Simply put, you have to be there.

The surprising (and probably disturbing) corollary to this is that we don't learn much about making art from being moved by it. Making art is bound by where we are, and the experience of art we have as viewers is not a reliable guide to where we are. As viewers we readily experience the power of ground on which we cannot stand — yet that very experience can be so compelling that we may feel almost honor-bound to make art that recaptures that power. Or more dangerously, feel tempted to use the same techniques, the same subjects, the same symbols as appear in the work that aroused our passion — to borrow, in effect, a charge from another time and place.

It's not hard to track the source of such desire: our most personal histories hold crystalline memories of absorption into evocative work. Sometimes such moments are part of why we become artists, and the works that moved us take on heroic importance. I can remember to within one heartbeat the moment I first saw an Edward Weston print. As I was walking the dim hallway that leads to the Rare Book Room of the UCLA Library, I glanced up — and saw this *photograph*. I stopped walking. Confusion. It was unlike anything else I had seen. It was so much more....*something*...than other photographs, particularly *my* photographs. *It was different in kind.* In that instant an unbidden distinction formed in my gut — there were now two kinds of photographs in the world: the one before me on the wall, and all the rest.

That photograph was mine to experience. But neither it, nor anything like it, was mine to make. Yet it took a decade to dispel the gnawing feeling that my work should do what that work had done. And more years still before I thought to question where the power of such art resided: In the maker? In the artwork? In the viewer?

If, indeed, for any given time only a certain sort of work resonates with life, then that is the work you need to be doing in that moment. If you try to do some other work, you will miss your moment. Indeed, our own work is so inextricably tied to time and place that we cannot recapture even our *own* aesthetic ground of past times. Try, if you can, to reoccupy your own aesthetic space of a few years back, or even a few months. There is no way. You can only plunge ahead, even when that carries with it the bittersweet realization that you have already done your very best work.

This heightened self-consciousness was rarely an issue in earlier times when it seemed self-evident that the artist (and everyone else, for that matter) had roots deeply intertwining their culture. Meanings and distinctions embodied within artworks were part of the fabric of everyday life, and the distance from art issues to all other issues was small. The whole population counted as audience when artists' work encompassed everything from icons for the Church to utensils for the home. In the Greek amphitheater twenty-two hundred years ago, the plays of Euripides' were performed as contemporary theatre before an audience of fourteen *thousand.* Not so today.

Today art issues have for the most part become solely the concern of artists, divorced from — and ignored by — the larger community. Today artists often back away from engaging the times and places of their life, choosing instead the largely intellectual challenge of engaging the times and places of Art. But it's an artificial construct that begins and ends at the gallery door. Apart from the readership of *Artforum,* remarkably few people lose sleep trying to incorporate gender-neutral biomorphic deconstructivism into their personal lives. As Adam Gopnik remarked in *The New Yorker*, "Postmodernist art is, above all, post-*audience* art."

In such a setting artists strain to find material of any human consequence. Under pressure of impending irrelevance, they may begin to fill their canvasses and monitors with charged particles "appropriated" from other places and times. It is as though art itself confers universality upon its subject, as though in art all objects automatically retain their power — as though you could incorporate the power of the Plains Indian medicine bundle into *your* work. Or convincingly complete the closing movements to Schubert's Unfinished Symphony. Today, indeed, you can find urban white artists — people who could not reliably tell a coyote from a german shepherd at a hundred feet — casually incorporating the figure of Coyote the Trickster into their work. A premise common to all all such efforts is that power can be borrowed across space and time. It cannot. There's a difference between meaning that is embodied and meaning that is referenced. As someone once said, no one should wear a Greek fisherman's hat except a Greek fisherman.

CANON

If you're like most artists we know, you're probably accustomed to watching your work unfold smoothly enough for long stretches of time, until one day — for no immediately apparent reason — it doesn't. Hitting that unexpected rift is commonplace to the point of cliché, yet artists commonly treat each recurring instance as somber evidence of their own personal failure. Nominees for Leading Role in a Continuing Artists' Funk are: (1) you've entirely run out of new ideas forever, or (2) you've been following a worthless deadend path the whole time. And the winner is: (fortunately) neither. One of the best kept secrets of artmaking is that new ideas come into play far less frequently than practical ideas—ideas that can be re-used for a thousand variations, supplying the framework for a whole body of work rather than a single piece. And likewise, fear that you've been following the wrong ideas is merely the downside variant of common fantasies about the way things could have been. The promise of paths not taken is that our work is really more than it appears, that it would shine through better if only things had been a little bit different. Confronting a disappointing piece, one somehow wants to disown it, to say, *"That's not what I meant to do; I should have made it larger, or maybe smaller; if only I'd had more time or money or hadn't used that stupid green paint..."* We'd all love to squirm out of this one, but the undeniable fact is that your art is not some residue left when you subtract all the things you haven't done—it is the full payoff for all the things you *have* done. One might as well wish for indulgence to go back and pick better numbers for last week's lottery.

Time travellers and tabloid psychics aside, the rest of us directly engage only today today. And when you watch your work unfold day by day, piece by piece, there's no escaping cause and effect. Simply put, what you did got you here, and if you apply the same methods again you will likely get the same result again. This is true not just for being stuck, but for all other artistic states as well — including highly productive states. As a practical matter, ideas and methods that work usually continue to work. If you were working smoothly and now you are stuck, chances are you unnecessarily altered some approach that was already working perfectly well. (For years I set aside daytimes for artmaking and evenings for writing; at some point I reversed that schedule, and months passed before I realized my writing had dried up—not for lack of ideas, but because it turns out I process words better at midnight than at midday.) When things go haywire, your best opening strategy might be to return—very carefully and consciously — to the habits and practices in play the last time you felt good about the work. Return to the space you drifted away from and (sometimes at least) the work will return as well.

And sometimes it won't. Artists (like everyone else) have a certain conceptual inertia, a tendency to keep to their own compass heading even as the world itself veers off another direction. When Columbus returned from the New World and proclaimed the earth was round, almost everyone else went right on believing the earth was flat. *Then they died*—and the next generation grew up believing the world was round. *That's* how people change their minds.

That's also to say that usually—but not always—the piece you produce tomorrow will be shaped, purely and simply, by the tools you hold in your hand today. In that sense the history of art is also the history of technology. The frescoes of pre-Renaissance Italy, the tempera paintings of Flanders, the *plein aire* oils of southern France, the acrylics of New York City—each successive technology imparted characteristic color and saturation, brushstroke and texture, sensuality or formality to the art piece. Simply put, certain tools make certain results possible.

Your tools do more than just influence the appearance of the resulting art—they basically set limits upon what you *can* say with an art piece. And when particular tools and materials disappear (because knowledge of how to make or use them is lost), artistic possibilities are lost as well. The sound of baroque instruments, the impression of the letterpress, the tonality of platinum prints—count these among the endangered species of artmaking. And likewise when new tools appear, new artistic possibilities arise. A scene painted *from life*, for instance, reveals a world far different from the one painted from memory. This became evident in the 1870's when manufacturers found a way to seal oil colors in collapsible metal-foil tubes, and for the first time artists working in that medium had the option of leaving the studio and painting with oils directly in the field. Some did, and some didn't. Those who did became known as the Impressionists.

The dilemma every artist confronts, again and again, is when to stick with familiar tools and materials, and when to reach out and embrace those that offer new possibilities. And on average, the younger artist tends to experiment with a large and varied range of tools and materials, while the veteran artist tends to employ a small and specific set. In time, as an artist's gestures become more assured, the chosen tools become almost an extension of the artist's own spirit. In time, exploration gives way to expression.

Either way, however, there is always one large obstacle to making mid-course corrections in our working methods: we hardly know what the methods themselves are. And when the work is going well, why on earth would we want to know? Most of the myriad of steps that go into making a piece (or a year's worth of pieces) go on below the level of conscious thought, engaging unarticulated beliefs and assumptions about what artmaking is. They remain as unknown and unconsidered as the steps we take in deciding whether to burnish the plate with straight or with circular strokes. Ask yourself why (for instance) you listen to country western music while you're painting? (Does it encourage you to choose brighter colors?) Why do you leave your studio unheated even when it means working with your overcoat on? (Does it make your brushstrokes crisper?) How do you sense when the dampened paper wants to take the watercolors? (By touch? Smell? The limpness of the paper?) We rarely think about how or why we do such things — we just do them. Changing the pattern of outcome in your work means first identifying things about your approach that are as automatic as wedging the clay, as subtle as releasing the arrow from the bow.

The details of artmaking we do recognize tend to be hard-won practical working habits, and recurrent bits of form that we can repeatedly hang work on. (Sometimes on dull days I've said to myself half-aloud that if I just go into the studio and start a wet piece, I'll at least have to finish *something* before it dries.) We use predictable work habits to get us into the studio and into our materials; we use recurrent bits of form as starting points for making specific pieces. Considering the number of Mazurkas he wrote, we have to think that once Chopin found that musical form he must have been a happier composer. It's easy to imagine that he could sit at the piano most any time and begin to vamp in that oddly syncopated three-quarter time, gradually building it into a small-scale piece. For Chopin that form was so conducive to exploration and variation he was able to reuse it for years. Equally, it must have been just plain helpful when J.S. Bach committed to writing a prelude and fugue in each of the twenty-four keys, since each time he sat down to compose he at least had a place to start. (*"Let's see, I haven't begun to work on the F-sharp minor yet..."*) Working within the self-imposed discipline of a particular form eases the prospect of having to reinvent yourself with each new piece.

The discovery of useful forms is precious. Once found, they should never be abandoned for trivial reasons. It's easy to imagine today's art instructor cautioning Chopin that the Mazurka thing is getting a little repetitive, that the work is not progressing. Well, true, it may not have been progressing—but that's not the issue. Writing Mazurkas may have been useful only to Chopin—as a vehicle for getting back into the work, and as a place to begin making the next piece. For most artists, making good art depends upon making lots of art, and *any* device that carries the first brushstroke to the next blank canvas has tangible, practical value.

Only the maker (and then only with time) has a chance of knowing how important small conventions and rituals are in the practice of staying at work. The private details of artmaking are utterly uninteresting to audiences (and frequently to teachers), perhaps because they're almost never visible—or even knowable—from examining the finished work. Hemingway, for instance, mounted his typewriter at counter-height and did all his writing while standing up. If he wasn't standing, he wasn't typing. Of course that odd habit isn't visible in his stories—but were he denied that habit, there probably wouldn't *be* any stories.

The hardest part of artmaking is living your life in such a way that your work gets done, over and over— and that means, among other things, finding a host of practices that are just plain useful. A piece of art is the surface expression of a life lived within productive patterns. Over time, the life of a productive artist becomes filled with useful conventions and practical methods, so that a string of finished pieces continues to appear at the surface. And in truly happy moments those artistic gestures move beyond simple procedure, and acquire an inherent aesthetic all their own. They are your artistic hearth and home, the working-places-to-be that link form and feeling. They become — like the dark colors and asymmetrical lilt of the Mazurka — inseparable from the life of their maker. They are canons. They allow confidence and concentration. They allow not knowing. They allow the automatic and unarticulated to remain so. Once you have found the work you are meant to do, the particulars of any single piece don't matter all that much.

PART II

When bankers get together for dinner, they discuss Art.
When artists get together for dinner, they discuss money.
— Oscar Wilde

VI.

A VIEW INTO THE OUTSIDE WORLD

To see far is one thing: going there is another.
— Brancusi

TO THE ARTIST, all problems of art appear uniquely personal. Well, that's understandable enough,
given that not many other activities routinely
call one's basic self-worth into question. But those really personal problems all relate to the making of the art.
Once the art has *been made,* an entirely new set of problems arise, problems that require the artist to engage
the outside world. Call them ordinary problems.

ORDINARY PROBLEMS

Ordinary problems are not, however, trivial problems. Among other things, they consume the larger
part of almost every artist's time. One well-known
painter, after several months of careful record keeping, reached the discouraging conclusion that even at
best he could free up only six or seven days a month

for actually *painting*, while the remaining twenty-odd days inevitably went to gallery business, studio clean-up, UPS runs and the like. Moral: There's one hell of a lot more to art than just making it. In many cases, the art you make today will reach its audience tomorrow only because of a vast societal network geared to arts education, funding, criticism, publication, exhibition and performance.

In many other cases, unfortunately, your art will only reach the world *in spite* of this network. Many attempts to introduce art to the larger world simply give evidence of the uneasy fit in our society between economics and beliefs. In many quarters art is viewed as dangerous, unnecessary, elitist, expensive — and dependent on the patronage of effete East Coast liberals for its survival. Artists themselves fare little better, being widely portrayed as subversive weirdos who not only enjoy Living In Sin, but are probably doing it off Your Tax Dollars as well!

> *Having said* that, *the authors would like to employ* this *sentence to proclaim a self-imposed moratorium on cynicism in their future discussions — regardless of how much the bastards deserve it. Thank You.*
> — THE MANAGEMENT

In any case, there's nothing obscure about either the cause or the effect of these attitudes. Some art, by its very nature, is subversive. By leading the viewer to experience the world through the very different sensibilities of the artist, a good work of art inevitably calls the viewer's own belief system into question. Is this threatening? *Is the Pope Catholic?* The more effective the art, the more likely the viewer's first reaction will be anger and denial — followed immediately by a search for someone to blame. And in that department the artist is always the most likely candidate — we have, after all, a time-honored tradition of killing the messenger who delivers the bad news.

One of the more celebrated examples of mowing down the messenger — and everyone else in sight — involved Robert Mapplethorpe, a photographer who made a set of images overtly romanticizing homosexuality. As it turned out, threats didn't mean a lot to Mapplethorpe, who was already terminally ill even as he readied this body of work for exhibit. Instead, pressure points were found in the supporting arts network, especially the National Endowment for the Arts. Subtlety was not in great abundance here: the NEA was simply threatened with a cutoff of funding if it lent support to artists or museums that made or exhibited work that offended "community standards".

There were counter-protests, of course, and in the end Mapplethorpe's work was exhibited, but the message to the arts community was clear: stray too far from the innocuous, and the axe would fall. Call it selective censorship: freedom of expression was guaranteed *unless* it was expressed in a work of art. The most amazing aspect of this American morality play was not that the government would place self-interest above principle when it felt threatened, but that no one foresaw this coming from miles down the road. A reminder from history: the American Revolution was not financed with matching Grants from the Crown.

COMMON GROUND

It goes without saying that censorship is debilitating to the artist. It's a little less obvious (at least to artists) that censorship is an entirely natural state of affairs. Nature places a simple constraint on those who leave the flock to go their own way: they get eaten. In society it's a bit more complicated. Nonetheless the admonition stands: avoiding the unknown has considerable survival value. Society, nature and artmaking tend to produce guarded creatures.

The dilemma here is that for the artist, contact with subject and materials must always remain *un*guarded. In making art you court the unknown, and with it the paranoia of those who fear what change might bring. But while fear of attracting the wrath of some southern Senator may cast a shadow on your freedom of expression, often the more vexing problem is catching anyone's attention in the first place. After all, most people see no reason to question their own beliefs, much less solicit yours.

And why should they? Artistically and otherwise, the world we come into has already been observed and defined by others—thoroughly, redundantly, comprehensively, and usually quite appropriately. The human race has spent several millennia developing a huge and robust set of observations about the world, in forms as varied as language, art and religion. Those observations in turn have withstood many — enormously many — tests. We stand heir to an unstatably large set of meanings.

Most of what we inherit is so clearly correct it goes unseen. It fits the world seamlessly. It *is* the world. But despite its richness and variability, the well-defined world we inherit doesn't quite fit each one of us, individually. Most of us spend most of our time in other peoples' worlds — working at predetermined jobs, relaxing to pre-packaged entertainment — and no matter how benign this ready-made world may be, there will always be times when something is missing or doesn't quite ring true. And so you make your place in the world by making part of it — by contributing some new part to the set. And surely one of the more astonishing rewards of artmaking comes when people make time to visit the world *you* have created. Some, indeed, may even purchase a piece of your world to carry back and adopt as their own. Each new piece of your art enlarges *our* reality. The world is not yet done.

ART ISSUES

It seems harmless enough to observe here that having an MFA (or even a knowledge of modern art) should hardly be a prerequisite to making art. After all, art appeared long before Art Departments, long before anyone began classifying or collecting artists' works. Nonetheless, most artists today do have formal training in art, a familiarity with the current art world trends, and at least some dependence on galleries or academia for their livelihood.

This is understandable (if not exactly healthy) given that each link in the arts network has a vested interest in defining its own role as fundamental and necessary. One of the ordinary problems artists face is finding a way to make peace with the arts network and the issues it holds dear. Not necessarily joining it, mind you — just making peace with it. At least you need to if you want assurance your work will likely be shown, published or performed in any reasonable length of time.

If the need to get shown is strong enough, this is not a problem. But the unease many artists feel today betrays a lack of fit between the work of their heart and the emotionally remote concerns of curators, publishers and promoters. It's hard to overstate the magnitude of this problem. Finding your place in the art world is no easy matter, if indeed there is a place for you at all. In fact one of the few sure things about the contemporary art scene is that someone besides you is deciding which art — and which artists — belong in it. It's been a tough century for modesty, craftsmanship and tenderness.

COMPETITION

There's no denying competition. It's hard-wired into us. It's *chemical*. Good athletes bank on that surge of energy that arises in the instant of knowing they can overtake the runner just ahead. Good artists thrive on exhibit and publication deadlines, on working twenty hours straight to see the pots are glazed and fired *just so*, on making their next work better than their last. The urge to compete provides a source of raw energy, and for that purpose alone it can be exceptionally useful. In a healthy artistic environment, that energy is directed inward to fulfill one's own potential. In a healthy artistic environment, artists are not in competition with each another.

Unfortunately, healthy artistic environments are about as common as unicorns. We live in a society that encourages competition at demonstrably vicious levels, and sets a hard and accountable yardstick for judging who wins. It's easier to rate artists in terms of the recognition they've received (which is easily compared) than in terms of the pieces they've made (which may be as different as apples and waltzes.) And when that happens, competition centers not on making work, but on collecting the symbols of acceptance and approval of that work—N.E.A. Grants, a Show at *Gallerie d'jour*, a celebrity profile in *The New Yorker* and the like.

Taken to extremes, such competition slides into needless (and often self-destructive) comparison with the fortunes of others. W.C. Fields became enraged at the mere mention of Charlie Chaplin's name; Milton suffered lifelong depression from ongoing self-comparison with Shakespeare; Solieri went a bit more insane each time he compared his music to Mozart's. (And who among us would welcome *that* comparison!?) Fear that you're not getting your fair share of recognition leads to anger and bitterness. Fear that you're not as good as a fellow artist leads to depression.

Admittedly, few of us are above feeling a momentary stab of pain when someone else wins the fellowship we sought, or a secret rush of triumph when we scoop up the same prize. (Kingsley Amis allowed that when he'd start writing a new novel, part of his motive was, "I'm going to show them, this time!") But occasional competitive grousing is a healthy step removed from equating success with standing atop the bodies of your peers. If nothing else it's hard to claim victory when your imagined competitors may be entirely unaware of your existence — after all, some may have already been *dead* for a century. Quite plausibly they don't win, while you — sooner or later — will lose. In some forms of comparison, defeat is all but inevitable.

But regardless of the yardstick used, all competitors share one telling characteristic: they know where they rank in the pack. Avid competitors check their ranking constantly. Obsessive competitors simply equate rank with self — a chancy gambit, but one that works (when it does work) by tapping a source of energy that makes them work harder at their art, and almost always makes them good careerists. When sense of self depends so directly upon the ranking bestowed by the outside world, motivation to produce work that brings high ratings is extreme. In not knowing how to tell yourself that your work is OK, you may be driven to the top of the heap in trying to get the rest of the world to tell you.

In theory this is a perfectly valid approach — the tricky part is finding the right yardstick for measuring your accomplishments. What makes competition in the arts a slippery issue is simply that there's rarely any consensus about what your best work *is*. Moreover, what's important about each new piece is not whether it is better or worse than your previous efforts, but the ways in which it is similar or different. The meaningful comparison between two Bach fugues is not how they rank, but how they work.

When things go really well in your artmaking, all the pieces you make have a life to them, regardless of how they stack up as personal favorites. After all, they're all your babies. It can even be argued that you have an obligation to explore the possible variations, given that a single artistic question can yield many right answers. Productive times encourage you to build an extended body of work, one where all the pieces (even the flawed sketches that will never see the gallery wall) have a chance to play. In healthy times you rarely pause to distinguish between internal drive, sense of craft, the pressure of a deadline or the charm of a new idea — they all serve as sources of energy in the pieces you make.

NAVIGATING THE SYSTEM

Artists, it turns out, are a crafty lot, and surprisingly adept at getting the system to foot the bill for letting them do exactly what they wanted to do anyway. Michelangelo painted the ceiling of the Sistine Chapel on commission from the Church; Ansel Adams photographed *Moonrise, Hernandez* on assignment for the Department of the Interior. Eames furniture and Avedon fashion spreads prove that art can prevail even at the extremes of commerce and fluff. Indeed, a disconcertingly strong argument can be made for the proposition that many artworks—especially large-scale efforts like the Parthenon or the Vietnam War Memorial—have had a buyer in place before the artwork was begun.

The problem is to keep such command performances from tainting the work that follows, since commissioned art has a way of sliding slowly and imperceptibly into commercial trade. This is especially troublesome for art forms that have widespread (and higher paying) commercial applications. The challenge in such circumstances is to convince the patron that you alone know the right way to make the piece.

For some artists it's a trade-off (or perhaps a standoff.) At Christmastime, ballet companies (even the major players) offer an inordinate number of performances of the *Nutcracker*, that being the only ballet that generates enough ticket sales to pull them through the rest of the season. Likewise printmakers, without altering the content of their work, learn soon enough which images will likely justify the cost of running a large edition.

For many other artists, however, the arts network proves an unmitigated disaster. Sometimes it's just that the freewheeling thought patterns that lead to art-making don't lead as gracefully to tidy record keeping. More often, though, the same artists who diligently follow a self-imposed discipline (like writing in iambic pentameter, or composing for solo piano) prove singularly ill-equipped to handle constraints imposed by others. Edward Weston's well-meaning friends once convinced a coffee company to offer that artist a commission to make still-life photographs they could use in their magazine ads. About the only requirement was that the company's product appear somewhere in the arrangement; nonetheless Weston, whose facility with photographing small objects as art is legendary, was driven to complete distraction by the pressure of having to make one of those small objects a coffee can.

Ideally (at least from the artist's viewpoint), the arts network is there to handle all those details not central to the artmaking process. This is a healthy attitude to nurture, since some art forms (like cinema and literature) could never make the leap from idea to reality without a sizeable investment from the outside anyway. Writers routinely mail out manuscripts and leave virtually all that follows — proofreading, design, printing, distribution and promotion — in the publisher's hands. Some artists even make the interface a prominent part of their work. Christo's various "wrappings" are a form of performance art experienced directly by relatively few people—but the *record* of the performance has become its own art piece, exhibited in museums complete with maps, working drawings, correspondence with zoning boards, logistical plans, and so on. If all this evidence of the reach of today's arts network still fails to impress you, consider the sobering corollary: once you're dead, *all* your art is handled by this network.

But if the artist stands as an endangered species in the face of contemporary economics and marketing, we are faced with a perplexing question: why does the myth of the individual artist — the loner following his/her own heart—arise so predictably with each new generation?

One possible answer is suggested by looking at the things that have made art worth doing in the past. Work that was driven by issues arising from the relationship between the artist and the work, or the artist and the materials, or the artist and the subject matter, rings true. Such work, regardless of whether it fits with then-contemporary attitudes, seems to continue to make sense over time.

A second answer, more tentative, taps into the deep wellsprings of art: utility and ritual. In very early times, these basic needs provided the cultural niche for art, while self-expression (even if unrecognized as such) served to integrate personal experience and skill with those larger goals. But ritual, which took form as painted bison on the cave wall and found its high flowering in the time of the great religions, has receded into secular fad and decoration. And utility, in whose service the early artist gave form to every object from obsidian arrowheads to fired clay pottery, has yielded to complexity and mass production. In our time, the cultural niche for art remains unfilled, while self-expression has become an end in itself. This may not be the healthiest of situations — but then again no one said we're living in the healthiest of times either.

VII.

THE ACADEMIC WORLD

*When my daughter was about seven years old,
she asked me one day what I did at work. I told
her I worked at the college — that my job was to
teach people how to draw.*
  *She stared back at me, incredulous, and said,
"You mean they* forget?*"*

— Howard Ikemoto

T HE AUTHORS would like to open this discussion
with a radical proposition — namely, that University art programs *do* serve some useful purpose. Admittedly not a large purpose. And generally not their stated purpose. But some purpose. Now that may not be exactly a ringing endorsement, but remember, we're talking here about a field whose most prominent graduates describe themselves as survivors of their formal education.

Indeed, the thought of working in the art education system — either as student or faculty — may sound about as attractive as standing beneath a steady drizzle of dead cats. Viewed from the outside, most schooling gives every appearance of being not only destructive to the individual, but irrelevant to the great sweep of history as well. Horror stories abound. We've all been emotionally singed by some counterpart to the third grade teacher who told certain kids they sang so badly they should just silently mouth the words of the Christmas Pageant. Or some art history teacher who dismissed Rock 'n Roll or filmmaking with the backhanded one-liner, "It isn't art."

Viewed from the inside, however — by those who grapple with educational issues on a day-to-day basis — things naturally get more complicated. And personal. The dilemma facing academia is that it must accommodate not only students who are striving to become artists, but also teachers who are struggling to remain artists.

FACULTY ISSUES

Ironically, the artist who would teach is often doomed before ever setting foot in the classroom. Appraisals of teaching ability get skewed during even the initial job selection process. Typical application forms allow few judgements about the quality of one's teaching, but routinely demand some arbitrary *amount* of same. This makes newly-minted MFA graduates the perennial cannon fodder of the college job market, where they're routinely axed before ever landing their first position. Moreover, the same system that ignores the potential of the newcomer often discounts the achievements of the veteran. The author recalls once serving on a university search committee while it compared two applications, one listing three years teaching for the local Parks & Recreation summer program, the other attesting to an equivalent tenure on the art faculty at Harvard. Under state hiring guidelines, we were required to accord the two records equal ranking — once the requirement for "three years teaching experience" had been met, discriminating on the basis of *quality* was specifically forbidden.

When teaching ability is relegated to a statistic, artistic ability becomes (somewhat surprisingly) an asset. (As an aside, universities rarely have trouble attracting good artists — art has the dubious distinction of being one profession in which you routinely earn more by teaching it than by doing it.) Final selection often turns on the strength of one's standing in the art world: an impressive record of exhibition and publication, strong critical reviews, recognition from peers, honorary grants or fellowships, long-term involvement in the arts community — all these things help. In the best of all worlds, this would be a fine criterion; in the academic world, it's a setup for disaster. Higher education may excel in attracting a first-class artist, but it's rarely capable of supporting one.

Viewing the scene neutrally — that is, at the purely structural level — the first breakpoint has simply to do with setting priorities. It is, after all, hard to imagine placing a full-time teaching career atop a full-time artmaking career without *something* going awry in the process. As the old proverb cautions: if you chase two rabbits, you catch neither.

Typically, the artmaking rabbit disappears first. If you teach, you know the pattern already. By the end of the school week, you've little energy left for any artmaking activity of more consequence than wedging clay or cleaning brushes. By the end of the term, nurturing unfinished work (and frayed relationships) may well take precedence over making any new art at all. The danger is real (and the examples many) that an artist who teaches will eventually dwindle away to something much less: a teacher who formerly made art. One-person shows become memories, older work shuttles around a circuit of perfunctory group shows, and finally things just trail off entirely. Like some perverse recycling process from a sci-fi novel, the same system that produces new artists, produces ex-artists.

Needless to say, this scenario is fairly depressing. It is, however, neither absolute nor inevitable. For that matter you might first ask yourself: What's wrong with producing less art? After all, your kids *are* important, your job *does* serve a useful purpose — they deserve your time and energy too. And beyond that, strategies do exist — artistic strategies, if you will — that allow for and even enhance your ability to make new art while working in an academic setting. One way or another, most all these strategies build upon the widespread consensus among artists that the single most redeeming feature of teaching is *teaching*.

If you teach, you know that you gain as much from the interchange as do your students. The classroom studio, after all, gives you a forum where ideas are the coin of the realm. It allows you to draw energy from young minds filled with potential. It gives you a role in shaping the next generation of art. It keeps you alive. Teaching is part of the process of being an artist.

The corollary here is that the greatest gift you have to offer your students is the example of your own life as a working artist. There's a story told about philosopher George Santayana — that while teaching at Harvard he was approached by a student who asked what courses he would be teaching the following term. Replied Santayana: "Santayana I, Santayana II, and a seminar in Santayana III".

It's that basic. Your life is a paradigm of the process of being an artist, a witness and record to the way time and circumstance, event and emotion, courage and fear surround the making of art. Your experiences provide an affirmation to younger artists that the path they have chosen does lead somewhere, and that you are all really fellow travellers, separated only by the time you've already travelled down that path. What good teachers offer their students is something akin to the vulnerability found in a personal relationship — a kind of artistic and intellectual intimacy that lets others see *how* they reached a specific point, not simply that they did reach it. It is that willingness to lay open the line that runs between their life and their art that gives meaning to technique, and empowerment to artistic goals that for the student may still lie many years distant. Learning is the natural reward of meetings with remarkable ideas, and remarkable people.

To share this as a teacher, your job above all is to maintain your autonomy — both as an artist and as a teacher. Maintaining that autonomy, however, is no easy matter. Obstacles to continued artmaking are sometimes hard-wired into academic policy. It is, for instance, the *law* in California that full-time instructors at state colleges be on campus every day of the week — even when they have no classes. With each day hopelessly fragmented, the large blocks of time essential to many artmaking processes are irretrievably lost. And beyond that, time for both teaching and artmaking must often be shored up against erosion from a steady river of administrative busywork. The magnitude of the problem varies widely. I recall that at the University of Oregon, Art Department meetings and memos routinely bled away twenty hours a week from otherwise useful time. I also recall (more fondly) that during an entire academic year at Stanford University, the Art Department scheduled exactly one meeting — and then cancelled it for lack of a quorum!

It's no fun fighting a two-front war, but one way or another you have to preserve time both for making art and for sharing that artmaking process with your students. Often the best strategy for cultivating quality time is to simply avoid like the plague all activities that *don't*. Artist/teacher Jack Welpott, who for many years ran the photography program at San Francisco State University, provided the classic model for this approach. When asked how he managed to teach effectively and make art prolifically in the face of full-time faculty duties, Welpott said, "From the day I was hired I began cultivating a reputation within the Art Department of being sort of a flake. I found that after a year or so of losing track of my committee assignments, forgetting to answer memos and missing departmental meetings — well, after while they just stopped *asking* me to do all those things."

STUDENT ISSUES

Idealism has a high casualty rate. The chances are (statistically speaking) that if you're an artist, you're also a student. That says something very encouraging about the desire to learn art — and something very ominous about the attrition rate of those who try. There is, after all, a deadly corollary: most people stop making art when they stop being students.

Given that rather sobering reality check, our initial proposition — that art education does serve some useful purpose — triggers a flurry of student-related questions. Like what exactly is that purpose? Why study art in an academic setting anyway? Or for that matter, what does it even mean to "study art"? Are you there to contemplate universal truths, explore new artistic frontiers, or breed fame and fortune?

This contest to define the best framework for helping artists learn has been going on for at least a couple of centuries now, and chances are—surprise!—that we won't suddenly resolve the issue in the next few sentences. You can corral good arguments, successful examples, prominent graduates — and insufferable converts—to champion any of a whole flock of possible pathways. Ideally your options range across colleges, art schools, workshops, apprenticeships, study tours, self-teaching and more. Empirically, they implode to a field of two: the University, and everything else.

It's largely a question of structure. The strength of the university lies in the fact that you can study art, physics, anthropology, psychology and literature *all at once*. The basic strength of the "everything else" — an apprenticeship, for instance — is that you can devote your energies solely to art *all the time*.

Not surprisingly, each approach also carries built-in limitations. The university may prove too large and impersonal to nurture a young artist through long periods of self-doubt before craft and vision take hold. In addition, many university art courses are electives, their focus and intensity diluted by non-majors who bring no personal investment to the subject. (If calculus were tailored as a "fun" elective for art majors, math majors would doubtless feel their studies were being retarded too!) Conversely, a workshop or small conservatory may focus so tightly on art that you lose touch with larger worlds you need to explore. And in any case the very structure that makes most art education *work* — a sheltered and supportive environment for artmaking, and an invitation to disengage (for a time) from the day-to-day treadmill of income production — vanishes instantly once you're out of school. The discouraging truth is that the rest of the world neither cares whether you make art, nor has much interest in buying it if you do. As far as most people are concerned, art may be acceptable as a profession, but certainly not as an occupation. (Or as one of the authors' students dolefully pointed out, "Most professions come with a salary.") Simply put, making art is not considered a *real* job.

But then, the role of the university has always been to provide an education, which is a small but significant step removed from providing training. Training prepares you for a job; an education prepares you for life. But if the university lays the foundation for rich and interdisciplinary achievement over the long run, it's notorious for providing few employable skills in the short run. Art critic A.D. Coleman tells the story of a university art teacher who was frequently asked by anxious parents whether there would be jobs awaiting their children upon graduation. Invariably the professor would reply, "Not as a direct result of anything they'll learn from me!" This approach, however truthful, is rarely reassuring: many students view graduating as tantamount to being pushed, unprepared, into some yawning abyss — forever.

That prospect is daunting enough that many artists drop out before ever completing their studies; others do graduate, but then — pressed by economics — find no way to continue artmaking afterwards. And yet others prolong the death-watch by entering graduate programs. The latter approach, placed atop fifteen-odd years of already-completed education, is superfluous at best and often actually harmful to the student's artmaking capacity. (Jerry Uelsmann refers to coaxing art from graduate students as a process of "rehabilitating the over-educated"!)

This whole scenario is a tragedy seldom addressed by academics, and even then is rarely acknowledged as a failure of the system. Watching from a safely tenured vantage point, the system instead laments the failure of the student. Poor therapists, I'm told, always blame their clients.

Faced with such poor odds for artistic survival (much less success), upper division students migrate in droves toward the one job for artists that society does validate: Teaching. This is a perilous course. There are many good reasons for wanting to teach, but avoiding the unknown is not one of them. The security of a monthly paycheck mixes poorly with the risk-taking of artistic inquiry.

The discouraging truth is that MFA degrees were created largely to provide — and then satisfy — a prerequisite for obtaining teaching jobs. This in effect rendered the entire system a pyramid scheme: it worked only so long as there were a dozen entering freshmen to match with each graduating MFA. For better or worse, this pyramid began crumbling years ago. Today art education is a steady-state universe, creating virtually no new jobs at all. Chances are — statistically speaking — that if you study art with a goal of teaching it, you'll end up with a career in sales. You study artmaking in order to learn about artmaking.

BOOKS ABOUT ART

Books on art, even books on artists, characteristically have little to say about actually *making* art. They may offer a sprinkling of romantic parables about "the artist's struggle", but the prevailing premise remains that art is clearly the province of genius (or, on occasion, madness). Accepting this premise leads inescapably to the conclusion that while art should be understood or enjoyed or admired by the reader, it most certainly should not be *done* by the reader. And once that kinship between reader and artist has been denied, art itself becomes a strange foreign object — something to be pointed to and poked at from a safe analytical distance. To the critic, art is a noun.

Clearly, something's getting lost in the translation here. What gets lost, quite specifically, is the very thing artists spend the better part of their lives doing: namely, learning to make work that matters to them. What artists learn from other artists is not so much history or technique (although we learn tons of that too); what we really gain from the artmaking of others is courage-by-association. Depth of contact grows as fears are shared — and thereby disarmed — and this comes from embracing art as process, and artists as kindred spirits. To the artist, art is a verb.

This distinction has substantial footing in the real world. Substantial enough at least to support the provocative — if not entirely airtight — proposition that *nothing* really useful can be learned from viewing finished art. At least nothing other artists can usefully apply in making their own art. The really critical decisions facing every artist — like, say, knowing when to *stop* — cannot be learned from viewing end results. For that matter, a finished piece gives precious few clues as to *any* questions the artist weighed while making the object.

You know how it is: in the heat of working, the thoughts in your head ricochet among a bewildering jumble of personal, shared and universal concerns. (But oh yes: for each artist, a very specific jumble!) And physically, you may be at your best when you're sweating in the sun, responding to a live audience, or — like the author as he writes this sentence — relaxing alone with a glass of wine. It's easy to imagine a hundred different states of mind that might have led Edward Weston to photograph his garden vegetables, but we have not the faintest possibility of knowing whether our best guess from that hundred matched his actual state. And equally poor prospects that the resulting print will provide any guide to understanding the state of mind that transformed pepper number thirty into *Pepper #30.*

This impasse may be what led Ezra Pound to remark that the one thing he learned from viewing a good piece of art was that the other artist had done his job well, and thus he [Pound] was freed to explore another direction. The art critic faces a more vexing dilemma: in a nutshell, he cannot explain the finished art piece from looking at the artist, and he cannot explain the artist by viewing the finished art piece. And so art is treated like some foreign object, analyzed from afar for its relationship to politics and culture and history and (incestuously) to other art movements. Or more drudgerously catalogued into successive styles, periods and "Masterworks." Textbooks compound the problem by reducing the history of art to the history of art *that can be reproduced.* VerMeer miniatures and Bierstadt murals are allotted identical quarter-page niches, and art that doesn't lend itself to halftoning disappears entirely.

We're not trying to set up straw men here, and certainly there's no harm in standing back occasionally to gain an overview of history (and fantasize about your place in it). The point is simply that none of this will help you to get the paint to fall to the canvas the way you need it to. None of this will tell you what it's like to set the hammer to the marble for the first time. None of this will convey the terror of walking onto the stage to face a thousand people. For the working artist, the very best writings on art are not analytical or chronological; they are autobiographical. The artist, after all, was *there*.

An ancient tenet in Chinese painting holds that the Master paints not the created thing, but the forces that created it. Likewise, the best writing about art depicts not the finished piece, but the processes that created it. In his *Daybooks*, Edward Weston offered an intimate account (too intimate, some would say) of the myriad of influences bracketing the moment of exposure. In *The Double Helix*, Watson & Crick recorded (in more restrained style) the conjecture and experiments that led to their discovery of the molecular structure of DNA. In *Daybook*, artist Anne Truitt began a one-year journal (which in due time stretched to seven) filled with wisdom and insight. Weston's passion, Watson's logic, Truitt's introspection: these are all driving mechanisms of process. Every artist has issues that lie similarly close to the heart. Every artist could write such a book. You could write such a book.

VIII.

CONCEPTUAL WORLDS

The answers you get
depend upon the questions you ask.
— Thomas Kuhn

WRITER HENRY JAMES once proposed three questions you could productively put to an artist's work. The first two were disarmingly straightforward: *What was the artist trying to achieve? Did he/she succeed?* The third's a zinger: *Was it worth doing?*

Those first two questions alone are worth the price of admission. They address art at a level that can be tested directly against real-world values and experience; they commit you to accepting the perspective of the maker into your own understanding of the work. In short, they ask you to respond to the work itself, without first pushing it through some aesthetic filter labelled Behaviorism, Feminism, Postmodernism or What-everism.*

But it's that third question — *Was it worth doing?* — that truly opens the universe. What *is* worth doing? Are some artistic problems inherently more interesting than others? More relevant? More meaningful? More difficult? More provocative? Every contemporary artist dances with such questions as these.

IDEAS & TECHNIQUE

Provocative art challenges not only the viewer, but also its maker. Art that falls short often does so not because the artist failed to meet the challenge, but because there was never a challenge there in the first place. Think of it like Olympic diving: you don't win high points for making even the *perfect* swan dive off the low board. There's little reward in an easy perfection quickly reached by many.

To resist models of perfection in art may seem strange, given their acceptance in so many other facets

---

* A FOOTNOTE: Frederick J. Crews is author of the definitive text on the perils of philosophical tunnel vision. In fact the title to his small volume is itself a classic:

THE POOH PERPLEX
— A Freshman Casebook —
In Which It is Discovered that the True Meaning of the Pooh Stories is Not as Simple as is Usually Believed,
But for Proper Elucidation Requires the Combined Efforts of Several Academicians of Varying Critical Persuasions

of living. Swan dives notwithstanding, the Olympic Games themselves are founded on the concept of great achievement within a strict framework. Honors in the hundred meter dash, after all, go not to the runner who displays some intriguing personal skip, but to the one who reaches the set goal first. The burden for the artist, as Anne Truitt observes in her *Daybook*, is that "The lawyer and the doctor *practice* their callings. The plumber and the carpenter *know* what they will be called upon to do. They do not have to spin the work out of themselves, discover its laws, and then present themselves turned inside out to the public gaze."

Clearly that is not an easy space to put yourself in. And indeed many artists don't. Artists who need ongoing reassurance that they're on the right track routinely seek out challenges that offer the clear goals and measurable feedback — which is to say, technical challenges. The underlying problem with this is not that the pursuit of technical excellence is wrong, exactly, but simply that making it the primary goal puts the cart before the horse. We do not long remember those artists who followed the rules more diligently than anyone else. We remember those who made the art from which the "rules" inevitably follow.

More insidiously, technical standards have a way of taking on all the trappings of aesthetic standards. There is widespread agreement, for instance, that it's a genuine challenge to impart rich blacks and subtle high values to a photographic print. At some point, however, this seemingly neutral observation gave rise (especially among West Coast landscape photographers) to a moral imperative that photographs *should* display such tonal perfection. As this genre established itself, criteria for judging a print increasingly concentrated on the virtuoso technical performance needed to produce the desired tones. Subtlety of tone became, often quite literally, the primary content. An equivalent fate befell much twentieth century symphonic music, which was seduced by arcane harmonic theory to the degree that its critical audience drifted progressively to other idioms (like jazz) that remained grounded in the rhythms of the real world.

To the viewer, who has little emotional investment in how the work gets done, art made primarily to display technical virtuosity is often beautiful, striking, elegant...and vacant. To the artist, who has an emotional investment in *everything*, it's more a question of which direction to reach. Compared to other challenges, the ultimate shortcoming of technical problems is not that they're hard, but that they're easy.

Artists, naturally, would be the last to admit that, if only because heroic accounts of grueling hours spent building the mold or casting the hot metal remain *de riguer* of artistic conversation. But while mastering technique is difficult and time-consuming, it's still inherently easier to reach an already defined goal — a "right answer" — than to give form to a new idea. It's easier to paint in the angel's feet to another's masterwork than to discover where the angels live within yourself. If technique were the core issue in art, our nominee for the Famous Artists Wax Museum would be the lifer at San Quentin who spent twenty years constructing a perfect replica of the Eifel Tower *from toothpicks*. (And well, yes, in its own way it was pretty impressive!) But that's not the way it works. Simply put, art that deals with ideas is more interesting than art that deals with technique.

CRAFT

Yes, there *is* a difference between art and craft—it's just that both terms are so overgrown with fuzzy definitions that drawing a clear distinction between them is close to impossible. We'll settle here for a fuzzy distinction.

Think of craft and you think of furniture shaped by Sam Maloof, of handmade clothing flaunted at Renaissance Faires, of everything made before the Industrial Revolution. Think of art and you think of *War and Peace,* a Beethoven concerto, the *Mona Lisa*. Both disciplines obviously yield good things, valuable things, sometimes tangibly useful things, and at first pass the distinction between them seems perfectly clear.

But is the *Mona Lisa* really art? Well then, what about an undetectably perfect *copy* of the *Mona Lisa*? That comparison (however sneaky) points up the fact that it's surprisingly difficult, maybe even impossible, to view any single work in isolation and rule definitively,

"This is art" or "This is craft." Striking that difference means comparing successive pieces made by the same person.

In essence, art lies embedded in the conceptual leap between pieces, not in the pieces themselves. And simply put, there's a greater conceptual jump from one work of art to the next than from one work of craft to the next. The net result is that art is less polished—but more innovative—than craft. The differences between five Steinway grand pianos—demonstrably works of consummate craftsmanship—are small compared to the differences between the five Beethoven Piano concerti you might perform on those instruments.

A work of craft is typically made to fit a specific template, sometimes a painstakingly difficult template requiring years of hands-on apprenticeship to master. It's staggering to realize that nearly all the truly great violins ever produced were made in the course of a few years by a few artisans living within a few blocks of each other. All this in a remote Italian village, three centuries ago. The accomplishments of Antonio Stradivari and his fellow craftsmen point up one real difference between art and craft: with craft, perfection *is* possible. In that sense the Western definition of craft closely matches the Eastern definition of art. In Eastern cultures, art that faithfully carries forward the tradition of an elder master is honored; in the West it is put down as derivative.

Yet curiously, the progression of most artists' work over time is a progression from art toward craft. In the same manner that imagination gives way to execution as any single work builds toward completion, an artist's major discoveries usually come early on, and a lifetime is then allotted to fill out and refine those discoveries. As the Zen proverb suggests, for the beginner there are many paths, for the advanced, few.

At any point along that path, your job as an artist is to push craft to its limits — without being trapped by it. The trap is perfection: unless your work continually generates new and unresolved issues, there's no reason for your next work to be any different from the last. The difference between art and craft lies not in the tools you hold in your hands, but in the mental set that guides them. For the artisan, craft is an end in itself. For you, the artist, craft is the vehicle for expressing your vision. Craft is the visible edge of art.

NEW WORK

In routine artistic growth, new work doesn't make the old work false — it makes it more artificial, more an act of artifice. Older work is ofttimes an embarrassment to the artist because it feels like it was made by a younger, more naive person — one who was ignorant of the pretension and striving in the work. Earlier work often feels, curiously, both too labored and too simple. This is normal. New work is *supposed* to replace old work. If it does so by making the old work inadequate, insufficient and incomplete — well, that's life. (Frank Lloyd Wright advised young architects to plant ivy all around their early buildings, suggesting that in time it would grow to cover their "youthful indiscretions.") Old work tells you what you were paying attention to then; new work comments on the old by pointing out what you were *not* previously paying attention to. Now this would all be smooth and lovely except that new work can turn to old work in an instant — sometimes, indeed, in the instant immediately following the work's completion. Savoring finished work may last only an eye-blink. This is certainly unpleasant — but it's a good sign.

CREA**VITY

Readers may wish to note that *nowhere* in this book does the dreaded the C-word appear. *Why should it?* Do only some people have ideas, confront problems, dream, live in the real world and breathe air?

HABITS

Habits are the peripheral vision of the mind. Churning away just below the level of conscious decision-making, they scan a situation with a conceptual eye to disregarding most of it. The theory is simple enough: respond automatically to the familiar, and you're then free to respond selectively to the unfamiliar. Applying that theory, however, is a bit dicier. Indulge too many habits, and life sinks into mind-dulling routine. Too few, and coping with a relentless stream of incoming detail overwhelms you (much as users of certain psychotropic drugs become mesmerized once they notice that every blade of grass is *growing*.)

It's all a matter of balance, and making art helps achieve that balance. For the artist, a sketchpad or a notebook is a license to explore — it becomes entirely acceptable to stand there, for minutes on end, staring at a tree stump. Sometimes you need to scan the forest, sometimes you need to touch a single tree — if you can't apprehend both, you'll never entirely comprehend either. To *see* things is to enhance your sense of wonder both for the singular pattern of your own experience, and for the meta-patterns that shape all experience. All this suggests a useful working approach to making art: notice the objects you notice. (*e.g.* Read that sentence again.) Or put another way: make objects that talk — and then listen to them.

Habits get a lot of bad press in the art world. Well, no surprises there — in a field where iconoclasts flourish and exploring new ideas is the order of the day, who wants to stay home with the familiar? Indeed, why should you? After all, if you're comfortable with what you're doing, you've probably been there before. Yet larger questions will never get engaged unless huge amounts of detail can be trusted to habit. If art is to nourish consciousness, habitual reactions must be encouraged as well as questioned. The need is to search among your own repeated reactions to the world, expose those that are not true or useful, and change them. The remainder are yours: cultivate them. In any case, you haven't much choice. As mathematician G.K.

Chesterton wryly noted, "You can free things from alien or accidental laws, but not from the laws of *their own nature*. Do not go about encouraging triangles to break out of the prison of their three sides; if a triangle breaks out of its three sides, its life comes to a lamentable end."

The trick, of course, is cultivating habitual gestures that are *yours*. Unfortunately the outside world is not overly charitable to the artist in this effort. Habits imprinted by genes, parents, church, jobs and relationships are called character traits. Habits acquired from other artists are called — depending on the form they take — affectation, derivation, plagiarism or forgery. Your authors find this judgement a trifle harsh, especially since it invalidates the very source artists most often draw from in their early artmaking.

The effect on the artist, however, isn't nearly so dire as critics would have it appear. Many people first respond deeply to art — indeed, respond deeply to the world — upon finding works of art that seem to speak directly to them. Small surprise, then, if upon setting out to make art themselves, they begin by emulating the art or artist that brought this revelation. Beethoven's early compositions, for instance, show the unmistakable influence of his teacher, Franz Joseph Haydn. Most early work, in fact, only hints at the themes and gestures that will — if the potential isn't squandered — emerge as the artist's characteristic signature in later, mature work. At the outset, however, chances are that whatever theme and technique attract you, someone has already experimented in the same direction. This is unavoidable: making any art piece inevitably engages the large themes and basic techniques that artists have used for centuries. Finding your own work is a process of distilling from each those traces that ring true to your own spirit.

Once developed, art habits are deep-seated, reliable, helpful, and convenient. Moreover, habits are stylistically important. In a sense, habits *are* style. The unconsidered gesture, the repeated phrasing, the automatic selection, the characteristic reaction to subject matter and materials—these are the very things we refer to as style. Lots of people, artists included, consider this a virtue. Viewed closely, however, style is not a virtue, it is an inevitability—the inescapable result of doing anything more than a few times. The habitual gestures of the artist appear throughout any body of work developed enough to be called a body of work. Style is not an aspect of good work, it is an aspect of *all* work. Style is the natural consequence of habit.

ART & SCIENCE

It is an article of faith, among artists and scientists alike, that at some deep level their disciplines share a common ground. What science bears witness to experimentally, art has always known intuitively—that there is an innate rightness to the recurring forms of nature. Science does not set out to prove the existence of parabolas or sine curves or *pi*, yet wherever phenomena are observed, *there they are*. Art does not weigh mathematically the outcome of the brushstroke, yet whenever artworks are made, archetypal forms appear. Charles Eames, when asked just how he arrived at the curves used in his famous molded plywood chair, was clearly baffled that anyone would ask such a question; finally he just shrugged and replied, "It's in the nature of the thing." Some things, regardless of whether they are discovered or invented, simply and assuredly feel right. What is natural and what is beautiful are, in their purest state, indistinguishable. Could you improve upon the Circle?

In the day-to-day world, however, improving the circle is different from, say, improving the wheel. Science advances at the rate that technology provides tools of greater precision, while art advances at the pace that evolution provides minds with greater insight—a pace that is, for better or worse, glacially slow. Thus while the stone tools fashioned by cave dwellers an Ice Age ago are hopelessly primitive by current technological standards, their wall paintings remain as elegant and expressive as any modern art. And while a hundred civilizations have prospered (sometimes for centuries) without computers or windmills or even the wheel, none have survived even a few generations without art.

All that is not meant to cast art and science into some sort of moral footrace, but simply to point out that — in art as well as in science—the answers you get depend upon the questions you ask. Where the scientist asks what equation would best describe the trajectory of an airborne rock, the artist asks what it would feel like to throw one.

"The main thing to keep in mind," as Douglas Hofstadter noted, "is that science is about *classes* of events, not particular instances." Art is just the opposite. Art deals in any one particular rock, with its welcome vagaries, its peculiarities of shape, its unevenness, its noise. The truths of life as we experience them — and as art expresses them — include random and distracting influences as essential parts of their nature. Theoretical rocks are the province of science; particular rocks are the province of art.

The richness of science comes from really smart people asking precisely framed questions about carefully controlled events — controlled in the sense that such random or distracting influences don't count. The scientist, if asked whether a given experiment could be repeated with identical results, would have to say yes — or it wouldn't be science. The presumption is that at the end of a scientific experiment neither the researcher nor the world have changed, and so repeating the experiment would necessarily re-produce the same result. Indeed, *anyone* performing the experiment correctly would get the same results — a circumstance that on occasion leads to multiple claims for the same discovery.

But the artist, if asked whether an art piece could be remade with identical results, would have to answer no — or it wouldn't be art. In making a piece of art, both the artist and the artist's world are changed, and re-asking the question — facing the next blank canvas — will always yield a different answer. This creates a certain paradox, for while good art carries a ring of truth to it — a sense that something permanently important about the world has been made clear — the act of giving form to that truth is arguably unique to one person, and one time. There is a moment for each artist in which a particular truth can be found, and if it is not found then, it will not ever be. No one else will ever be in a position to write *Hamlet*. This is pretty good evidence that the meaning of the world is made, not found. Our understanding of the world changed when those words were written, and we can't go back...any more than Shakespeare could.

The world thus altered becomes a different world, with our alterations being part of it. The world we see today is the legacy of people noticing the world and commenting on it in forms that have been preserved. Of course it's difficult to imagine that horses had no shape before someone painted their shape on the cave walls, but it is not difficult to see the world became a subtly larger, richer, more complex and meaningful place as a result.

SELF-REFERENCE

Self-reference, repetition, parody, satire — art is nothing if not incestuous. Witness Escher's drawing of hands drawing hands. Twentieth century art has made self-reference pretty much its stock in trade — paintings about painting, writings about writing. Moreover, most every piece of art quotes itself, calling out its own name through rhythm and repetition. Music offers the clearest examples — like Beethoven building the first movement of his Fifth Symphony around just four notes — but all media have their equivalents.

When not quoting itself, artworks often pay homage to art that preceded them: Shostakovitch's masterful viola sonata (*Opus 147*) quotes Beethoven's *Moonlight Sonata,* wrapping the tune around itself, drawing attention to itself drawing attention to something else. At the less reverent level, this becomes satire and parody, as in Woody Allen's *Play It Again, Sam.*

An operation like (for instance) applying paint says something not only about itself, but about all the other applied paint as well. Rembrandt's work looks different — the paint more deliberately applied — after you've seen Jackson Pollock's. It looks even more different after you've applied paint yourself. Our understanding of the past is altered by our experiences in the present.

Turning the reference point inward, it's apparent that at some level, all art is autobiographical. After all, your brush only paints a stroke in response to your gesture, your word processor only taps out a sentence in response to your keystrokes. As Tennessee Williams observed, even works of demonstrable fiction or fantasy remain *emotionally* autobiographical. John Szarkowski once curated a show at the Museum of Modern Art titled *Mirrors and Windows*. His premise was that some artists view the world as if looking through a window at things happening "out there", while others view the world as if looking in a mirror at a world inside themselves. Either way, the autobiographical vantage point is implicit.

If art is about self, the widely accepted corollary is that making art is about self-expression. And it is—but that is not necessarily all it is. It may only be a passing feature of our times that validating the sense of who-you-are is held up as the major source of the need to make art. What gets lost in that interpretation is an older sense that art is something you do out in the world, or something you do about the world, or even something you do *for* the world. The need to make art may not stem solely from the need to express who you are, but from a need to complete a relationship with something outside yourself. As a maker of art you are custodian of issues larger than self.

Some people who make art are driven by inspiration, others by provocation, still others by desperation. Artmaking grants access to worlds that may be dangerous, sacred, forbidden, seductive, or all of the above. It grants access to worlds you may otherwise never fully engage. It may in fact be the engagement — not the art — that you seek. The difference is that making art allows, indeed guarantees, that you declare yourself. Art is contact, and your work necessarily reveals the nature of that contact. In making art you declare what is important.

METAPHOR

*When you start on a long journey, trees are trees,
water is water, and mountains are mountains. After
you have gone some distance, trees are no longer
trees, water no longer water, mountains no longer
mountains. But after you have travelled a great
distance, trees are once again trees, water is once
again water, mountains are once again mountains.*

— Zen teaching

Making art depends upon noticing things — things
about yourself, your methods, your subject matter.
Sooner or later, for instance, every visual artist notices
the relationship of the line to the picture's edge. Before
that moment the relationship does not exist; afterwards
it's impossible to imagine it *not* existing. And from that
moment on every new line talks back and forth with
the picture's edge. People who have not yet made this
small leap do not see the same picture as those who
have — in fact, conceptually speaking, they do not even
live in the same world.

Your work is the source for an uncountably large
number of such relationships. And these relationships,
in turn, are a primary source of the richness and complexity in your art. As your art develops, conceptual
relationships increasingly define the shape and
structure of the world you see. In time, they *are* the
world. Distinctions between you, your work and the
world lessen, grow transparent, and finally disappear.
In time, *trees are once again trees.*

Viewed over a span of years, changes in one's art often reveal a curious pattern, swinging irregularly between long periods of quiet refinement, and occasional leaps of runaway change. (And though it's beyond our purposes here, we can't help but note the tantalizing similarity between this pattern and the manifestations of chaos theory in mathematics.) Sometimes our perception of the world flows smoothly and continuously from one state to the next, and sometimes it flips over unexpectedly (and irrevocably) into a different configuration entirely. As schoolkids we memorize the famous examples—like Newton's apple delivering him the Law of Gravity—but always with the caveat that such events are rare, probably excessively rare. After all, how often does anyone get the chance to rewrite the underlying laws of physics?

Yet it's demonstrably true that all of us do (from time to time) experience such conceptual jumps, and while ours may not affect the orbit of planets, they markedly affect the way we engage the world around us. Study French, for instance, and you'll likely spend the first month painstakingly translating it word by word into English to make it understandable. Then one day—voilá!—you find yourself reading French *without* translating it, and a process that was previously enigmatic has become automatic. Or go mushroom hunting with someone who really knows mushrooms, and you'll first endure some downright humiliating outings in which the expert finds all the mushrooms and you find none. But then at some point the world shifts, the woods magically fill—mushrooms everywhere!—and a view that was previously opaque has become transparent.

For the artist, such lightning shifts are a central mechanism of change. They generate the purest form of metaphor: connections are made between unlike things, meanings from one enrich the meanings of the other, and the unlike things become inseparable. Before the leap there was light and shadow. Afterwards, objects float in a space where light and shadow are indistinguishable from the object they define.

Recently a painter of some accomplishment (but as insecure as the rest of us) was discussing his previous night's dream with a friend over coffee. It was one of those vivid technicolor dreams, the kind that linger on in exact detail even after waking. In his dream he found himself at an art gallery, and when he walked inside and looked around he found the walls hung with paintings — amazing paintings, paintings of passionate intensity and haunting beauty. Recounting his dream, the artist ended fervently with, "I'd give anything to be able to make paintings like that!"

"Wait a minute!" his friend exclaimed. "Don't you see? Those *were* your paintings! They came from your own mind. Who else could have painted them?"

Who else indeed?

Of course you can deny your dreams, but the result will be uniformly dreary. Insist that the world must always remain x, and x is indeed exactly what you'll get. But that's all the world will ever be. And all your art will ever be. When your only tool is a hammer, so the saying goes, everything looks like a nail. Imagination and execution take their rightful common ground in possible acts: paintable pictures, danceable steps, playable notes. Your growth as the artist is a growth toward fully realizable works — works that become real in full illumination of all that you know. Including all you know about yourself.

IX.

THE HUMAN VOICE

Computers are useless —
all they can give you are answers.
— Pablo Picasso

THROUGHOUT MUCH OF THIS BOOK we've tried to confront the difficulties of making art by examining the way those difficulties really happen in the studio. It's a simple premise: follow the leads that arise from contact with the work itself, and your technical, emotional and intellectual pathway becomes clear. Having come this far, it's tempting to try to bring this idea to closure by resolving all those leads into a single clear, concise, fundamental, finely honed *answer*. Tempting, but futile. Answers are reassuring, but when you're onto something really useful, it will probably take the form of a *question*.

QUESTIONS

Over the long run, the people with the interesting answers are those who ask the interesting questions.

Sometimes (and probably far more often than we realize), the really important questions roll around in our minds for a long time before we act upon them. Sometimes, in fact, they sit there for a long time before we even realize they're important. The question that probably served as the seed crystal for this book was posed to the authors nearly twenty years earlier. The occasion was a friendly debate surrounding the formation of a small artists' collective. The question was: *Do artists have anything in common with each other?*

Like any good question, that one quickly generated a flurry of relatives: *How do artists become artists? How do artists learn to work on their work? How can I make work that will satisfy me?* For young artists filled with energy and idealism, the answers seemed just around the corner. Only as the years passed did we begin to encounter, with increasing frequency, a much darker issue: *Why do so many who start, quit?*

Taken together, this cluster of questions marks the central pivot of *Art & Fear*. It's an odd cluster — not arcane enough, perhaps, to interest scholars, but too elusive to attract pop psychologists. Perhaps that's just as well. We live in a world where the ready-made observations about artmaking are typically useless, frequently fatalistic.

Q: *Will anyone ever match the genius of Mozart?*
A: *No.*
Thank you — now can we get on with our work?

Equally, there is no ready vocabulary to describe the ways in which artists become artists, no recognition that artists must learn to be who they are (even as they cannot help being who they are.) We have a language that reflects how we learn to paint, but not how we learn to paint *our* paintings. How do you describe the [*reader to place words here*] that changes when craft swells into art?

Artists come together in the clear knowledge that when all is said and done, they will return to their studio and practice their art alone. Period. That simple truth may be the deepest bond we share. The message across time from the painted bison and the carved ivory seal speaks not of the differences between the makers of that art and ourselves, but the similarities. Today those similarities lay hidden beneath urban complexity — audience, critics, economics, trivia — in a self-conscious world. Only in those moments when we are truly working on our own work do we recover the fundamental connection we share with all makers of art. The rest may be necessary, but it's not art. Your job is to draw a line from your life to your art that is straight and clear.

CONSTANTS

To a remarkable degree the outside world consists of variables and the interior world consists of constants. The constants are, well, *constant*: barring mental breakdown or a rare tropical fever, you'll carry the same burdens tomorrow and next year as you do today. We experience life as artists no differently from the way we experience life in any other role — we simply *exist*, perhaps watching from an imaginary point a little behind our eyes, while the scene we observe from that steady vantage point changes constantly.

This sense of interior stability is consistent with one widely observable truth: the arc to any individual life is uniform over long periods of time. Subjects that draw us in will continue to draw us in. Patterns we respond to we will continue to respond to. We are compelled by forces that, like the ocean current, are so subtle and pervasive we take them utterly for granted. Those odd moments when we notice the sea we swim in leave us as surprised as the discovery by Moliere's character that he was speaking prose, that indeed he had *always* spoken prose.

The artistic evidence for the constancy of interior issues is everywhere. It shows in the way most artists return to the same two or three stories again and again. It shows in the palette of Van Gogh, the characters of Hemingway, the orchestration of your favorite composer. We tell the stories we have to tell, stories of the things that draw us in — and why should any of us have more than a handful of those? The only work really worth doing — the only work you *can* do convincingly — is the work that focuses on the things you care about. To not focus on those issues is to deny the constants in your life.

116

VOX HUMANA

To make art is to sing with the human voice. To do this you must first learn that the only voice you need is the voice you already have. Art work is ordinary work, but it takes courage to embrace that work, and wisdom to mediate the interplay of art & fear. Sometimes to see your work's rightful place you have to walk to the edge of the precipice and search the deep chasms. You have to see that the universe is not formless and dark throughout, but awaits simply the revealing light of your own mind. Your art does not arrive miraculously from the darkness, but is made uneventfully in the light.

What veteran artists know about each other is that they have engaged the issues that matter to them. What veteran artists share in common is that they have learned how to get on with their work. Simply put, artists learn how to proceed, or they *don't*. The individual recipe any artist finds for proceeding belongs to that artist alone — it's non-transferable and of little use to others. It won't help you to know exactly what Van Gogh needed to gain or lose in order to get on with his work. What *is* worth recognizing is that Van Gogh needed to gain or lose at all, that his work was no more or less inevitable than yours, and that he — like you — had only himself to fall back on.

Today, more than it was however many years ago, art is hard because you have to keep after it so consistently. On so many different fronts. For so little external reward. Artists become veteran artists only by making peace not just with themselves, but with a huge range of issues. You have to find your work all over again all the time, and to do that you have to give yourself maneuvering room on many fronts — mental, physical, temporal. Experience consists of being able to reoccupy useful space easily, instantly.

In the end it all comes down to this: you have a choice (or more accurately a rolling tangle of choices) between giving your work your best shot and risking that it will not make you happy, or not giving it your best shot — and thereby *guaranteeing* that it will not make you happy. It becomes a choice between certainty and uncertainty. And curiously, uncertainty is the comforting choice.

About this Book

Evidently (since you're reading it) this book did get done, though describing just how it got done is a difficult proposition. The literal answer would probably be *slowly*, given that these words mark the end-point to seven years of more-or-less continuous work on this manuscript. Viewed from our perspective, however, this seems an entirely natural pace. Having already been friends for a whole bunch of years allowed for a genuinely enjoyable collaboration, one in which writing became a tool for clarifying issues we had often grappled with in friendly conversation.

Occasionally (when things were really slow) we tried to nudge the manuscript along by working in ways that one imagines collaborators working: agreeing to schedules, selecting topics to work on, or even meeting together in the presence of a tape recorder to preserve the fleeting ideas of long conversations. Like many other perfectly good theories, that one didn't work. In the end the work got done the way such things always get done — by carving out solo time for the project and nibbling away at it one sentence at a time, one idea at a time.

Like most projects, this one also managed to illuminate (in abundance) the familiar perils of artmaking. Despite our long friendship and despite ongoing conversations about the issues addressed here, our strengths proved to be more complementary than similar, resulting in roles that could never be reversed (and in fact were never even negotiated). We settled into the right pattern of collaboration, after a little fumbling, by simply letting well enough alone — working in parallel rather than in tandem, with each of us engaging the issues we were drawn to. Since artists rarely discuss this topic, however, we really don't know how closely our large (but not entirely matching) mix of vision, blindness, and willingness to look the other way resembles other collaborative efforts.

We have been helped throughout this project by many friends and fellow travellers — most of whom are probably unaware of their contribution. There was also knowing help early on from Spencer Bayles, Frances Orland, Steve Sturgis, Linda Jones and Keith Milman, which we greatly appreciated. We would especially like to thank Dave Bohn, who consistently challenged our thinking by raising large questions (and essential details) with abundant force and precision.

And lastly, we are greatly indebted to Noel Young of Capra Press for graciously accepting this book for publication even though *none* of us could figure out which shelf it belongs on in the bookstore, and to his assistant David Dahl for his endless patience and goodwill in fielding our many questions and requests in the succeeding years. It was only after Capra Press closed its doors for good in 2001 that we began publishing *Art & Fear* under our own imprint, Image Continuum Press.

David Bayles
Ted Orland

FROM THE SAME AUTHORS...

NOTES ON A SHARED LANDSCAPE
Making Sense of the American West
by David Bayles
FIRST PRINTING MAY 2005 • $29.95 HARDCOVER

In this superbly crafted collection of personal writings and photographs, David Bayles explores the bungled love affair between Euro-Americans and the western landscape that ironically continues to infatuate them. William Kittredge, whose books include *Who Owns The West?*, recognizes Bayles as a "longtime traveler in the dry interior west...who is profoundly conversant with the region's watersheds, ecosystems and cultures", and concludes, "This is a book anybody who is thinking seriously about the West ought to read and re-read. ...It's honest and useful. That's my idea of high praise."

THE VIEW FROM THE STUDIO DOOR
How Artists Find Their Way in An Uncertain World
by Ted Orland
FIRST PRINTING APRIL 2006 • $12.95 SOFTCOVER

In this perfect companion piece to *Art & Fear*, Ted Orland argues that when it comes to artmaking, theory and practice are inseparably linked. In a text marked by grace, brevity and humor, Orland connects the line between timeless philosophical questions about the underlying nature of art making (*How do we make sense of the world?*), and gritty real-world issues that artists confront the moment they're off the starting blocks and producing work on a regular basis (*Is there art after graduation?*). Think of it as practical philosophy for the working artist.